THE CODEPENDENT CHURCH

The Codependent Church

Virginia Curran Hoffman

CROSSROAD • NEW YORK

1991

The Crossroad Publishing Company
370 Lexington Avenue, New York, NY 10017

Printed in the United States of America
Typesetting output: TEXSource, Houston

Library of Congress Cataloging-in-Publication Data

Hoffman, Virginia.
    The codependent church / by Virginia Hoffman.
      p. cm.
    Includes bibliographical references.
    ISBN 0-8245-1115-8
    1. Church renewal. 2. Twelve-step programs—Religious aspects—
Christianity. 3. Non-institutional churches. I. Title.
BV600.2.H573 1991
243.8'6—dc20
                                  91-21870
                                  CIP

For all the women and men
of the Table Talk groups,
of the Twelve Step groups,
of base communities and house churches,
and all others who have been
a source of strength
and com-panions — sharers of bread,
on the journey;

and for my children,
Amy, Rebecca, Joseph, and Stephen,
that their journey to personal wholeness
may be a shorter, surer path
than my own.

Contents

PART IV
Recovery

Introduction

I do not think anyone writes about codependence as a matter of pure theory, but from the experience of trying to work through the problem. Codependence has been a struggle for me, both in church and in personal relationships. I began to study family systems as a personal quest, and then discovered that the same dynamics were occurring in church.

Many of us are striving toward a living church of mutually respectful, co-responsible adults; but since we go about it by focusing on others and trying to convince them to change — the methods of codependence — we maintain the one up, one down, parent-child model of church.

About ten years ago, I was attempting, in true codependent fashion, to convince a clergyperson with "power" to lend support to a plan originated by "lay" persons. The endeavor lasted almost a year. I drove many miles, conducted interviews over the entire metropolitan area at this person's request, and faithfully reported the results to him. In return, I received nothing but evasive answers to my requests and more assignments to complete. Throughout that period, as I recognized later, I was manipulated but I did not see it, was lied to and believed the lies. I thought all along that I was "reaching him."

I did not recognize that old futile pattern as "codependence" until the spring of 1987, just before I finished writing *Birthing a Living Church*. Two friends were trying to "convert" their pastors to a new process of Christian initiation. Their stories and their frustration sounded like the stories of spouses of addicts. It occurred to me that the attitudes and behavior patterns common to church "families" are very similar to the attitudes and behavior patterns of addictive family systems.

The paradox of addictive systems is that what people do to help the addict actually prevents that person from feeling the need to change; what they do from motives of love and loyalty actually prolongs the destruction of both the addict and the family.

The addictive family systems model is only one possible model for

9

studying church, and it does not answer all the problems that face us, but it does allow us to recognize a familiar dynamic, to let go of some truly destructive habits, and to concentrate our efforts on what truly is our responsibility.

Many people do not face their own codependent issues until middle age, when things begin to fall apart, when "covering up" does not cover enough. We are at such a crisis point with church. We are trying to find our way out of the mess, but instead are wandering in circles through the same old problems of power and fear. The addictive systems perspective on the problem and the addictions recovery model for resolution provide healthy and responsible alternatives to our present quandary.

It is futile to assign blame here, because each generation learns the unhealthy behavior from the generation before, and because even the most destructive addictive behavior seems to the addict to be necessary for self-defense and self-preservation. It is self-defeating to assign blame, because as long as we keep our focus on "them," we allow ourselves to believe that we cannot live healthy lives until *they* change.

We cannot blame, but until we admit that we are blinded by our own delusion that we can *own* God, and crippled by the constraints which that delusion puts on our thoughts and activities, we cannot ask for healing. If we could see more clearly, we would see that we do have choices.

The reason we *need* to take a look at these issues is not because we do not love the church, but precisely because we do love the church and do not want to contribute to any more sickness and pain.

I work out of a simple vision of church — I wrote *Birthing a Living Church* to describe that — and instead of pouring all my energy into trying to change the vision of others or trying to win their permission to act, I try to spend my energies where they can be more directly productive. I coordinate an interdenominational ministry center where people in the area can study and learn together and build networks of fellowship and support. The center runs on volunteer power, on the energy that had been held bound by codependence.

Codependence is not a black-and-white issue; it is a matter of degrees. We are more or less affected by this problem. Some may find that, in most areas of your religious experience, your attitudes and actions are healthy; others may discover that in one or two areas you are handicapped by codependence; some may even recognize a more serious problem. I hope, in any case, that this book will illuminate the problem and offer some help for recovery.

The book begins with the more recent insights on codependence and an application to church. There are two critical issues that seem to keep us codependent — sex and power — and so there are whole sections devoted to each of these. The last section considers alternative understandings and behaviors, other ways we might approach the process of becoming church.

Read "church" here in any way that speaks to your experience: it can be a faith community of any size or scope, from a small group meeting in a home to any international denomination. Any community can operate in unhealthy ways, and, as is true of families that exhibit these traits, some do so more than others.

My hope for those who read this is that you will know that you are not alone or crazy for thinking what you think or feeling what you feel, that others of us share the same perceptions. You do have a choice to re-vision church and to act responsibly out of that simpler vision. I hope, too, that you will get the help and support you need on your own journey of recovery, and that you will share what you learn with others.

I owe an apology to the reader who may be bothered by pronouns of one gender or the other. Addictions and codependence are equal-opportunity disabilities: anyone of any race, gender, or age may experience them. Unfortunately, we do not have a third-person singular personal pronoun that is neither male nor female, and friends said the use of "s/he" was very difficult to read. So, where I have had to use one or the other, I understand and I hope you understand that the other could be substituted as well.

I want to thank all who have contributed their own experiences of the codependent church, who have written their stories, who have shared and wrestled with the ideas, or who have read and evaluated individual chapters. I promised them anonymity when I asked for their help; their names will not appear here for their own protection. But I am grateful for their sense of church and for the assistance they have given me in this project.

There are many friends who have supported me in my own recovery from codependence, who have been church to me, who have given moral support, encouragement, and suggestions throughout the process of writing — I thank God for you all. Mary Bodin shared the peace of the Upper Room so the work could begin. Linda and Bill Dunn reviewed the entire manuscript and offered many valuable suggestions. The work is the better for the assistance of all these friends, though I would not want them judged for any deficiencies that remain.

Michael Leach, my publisher at Crossroad, continued to offer patience and confidence as I struggled past deadlines. I am so thankful for that support.

Part I

The Gospel of Codependence

1

Persons without Centers

Codependence is an unhealthy pattern of relating based on low self-esteem and on the belief that one's worth depends on attachment to, or the approval of, some other person or group.

When this term first came into use in the 1980s, it was thought that codependence occurred in adulthood as a result of living with an addict. It seemed that exposure to addictive behavior — rages one day, gifts and manipulation the next — would condition the healthy partner to check the mood of the addict before doing or saying anything, that years of measuring decisions against someone else would eventually cost the healthy partner all sense of self and initiative.

Long-term therapy with children, however, has indicated that the loss of self happens much earlier. The unhealthy pattern of behavior develops in childhood as a set of survival tools for dealing with stresses in dysfunctional families. "Dysfunctional" describes any families that are unable to provide the emotional bonding and nurturing necessary for the development of healthy and whole members. These include families in which one member is addicted (whether that person uses food, work, shopping, gambling, sex, drugs, alcohol, or any other substance or process as their anesthetic of choice), or families where one parent is emotionally absent, or where the family rules are so repressive that they prevent the development of healthy individuality.

This pattern was first recognized in addictive families. Studies of the inner workings of these systems provide valuable insights into the way codependence develops.

The Core Beliefs behind Addiction

Patrick Carnes identified four basic beliefs that form the worldview of all addicts and motivate their addictive behavior. They create the treadmill on which addicts — and their whole addictive family systems — seem to run. These core beliefs are:

1. I am no good.

2. No one would like me if they knew me as I am.

3. My needs will never be met if I have to depend on others.

4. My "fix" — whatever is the object of their compulsion — is my most important need. (*Out of the Shadows*, 82–85)*

The addict is hurting, but completely cut off from any help.

Craig Nakken paints a clear picture of the path to addiction (*The Addictive Personality: Roots, Rituals and Recovery*). A young person happens upon some mood-changing experience — beer, gambling, binge-eating, masturbation — that lifts him out of any pain he is feeling, at least temporarily. Addicts recall that their first experience with their anesthetic of choice was particularly intense, that it affected them differently than it seemed to affect others. If the young person has already acquired the four negative core beliefs, the discovery becomes all the more significant. That mood-altering experience makes him aware that there is an escape from his misery, that the escape is available to him at any time, and that it is not dependent on anyone else.

He begins to choose deliberately this means of escape, at first only in especially stressful situations, then more regularly. Over time, he has less and less control over the choice; it does not thrill as much, but he needs it to feel good, or even to feel "normal." The addiction takes over like another personality: it rationalizes situations, makes choices, covers up the addiction, and pushes others away so that they cannot interfere.

The behavior of addicts is very erratic: severely critical of others, of themselves, and of life in general as they "talk themselves into" acting out; abusive or oblivious of others while under the influence; or buying back or otherwise conning the family afterward. Life with an addict is life on a roller-coaster.

---

* Full bibliographical information for the references is provided in the Suggested Readings section at the end of the book.

Picture a household in which one of the parents is an active addict; it does not matter what the drug or process of choice is. This person has a young child, who has tried repeatedly to get close to the parent. Since the parent feels no good and is certain that no one could love him as he really is, he makes sure the child does not see him as he really is: he remains distant and superficial. The child wants to share something that happened at school — a friend treated her badly on the playground — but the parent, who probably never had a caring listener in his own childhood, is unable to listen, cannot affirm the child's feelings, and only offers a curt remark, "Life's tough all over." Often the parent is barricaded behind anesthetic effects of his own addiction and will not make any connection with the child at all.

What happens to that child, growing up with a parent who is driven by those damaging core beliefs and by an insatiable need for some addictive drug or process? Since children depend on their parents for survival, they learn to compensate for the unstable situation. They cannot admit the possibility that their parent might be wrong, or even dangerous. They conclude instead that their parent is good, but that *their own* actions must cause their parent to act out. They learn to monitor the moods of the addict and to adjust their own behavior to make up for their parent's, to do anything their parent might like or need so that that parent will not go away.

Living in this environment, the child comes to assume that she is no good: nothing she does can stop the addiction. Since the parent who knows her so well does not seem to care for her, she concludes that no one who knows her will ever like her for herself. She will learn that she cannot count on anyone to be there for her. And, when she happens to find something that can provide an escape from that grim existence — some anesthetic substance or process, finding and taking care of emotionally distant persons like her parent, or even working for the church — that something will become the "magic medicine" that can "make everything better" every time she uses it.

Life in the Church Family

We have been looking at families, and most studies focus on families, but the family is not the single source of codependent behavior. Church families, too, can teach us to be codependent. (Throughout this book, "church" is used to denote a religious group of any size or scope, from a house church to an international denomination.) Someone growing up in a closed and rigid Christian denomination might have been taught from tender years the same set of core beliefs that the addict holds: I am no good, steeped in sin from birth; no one would like me, not even God, the way I am; I cannot depend on anyone to be there for me — to listen to my fears and uncertainties, or to pay attention when I try to express my needs.

They learn that only the church can deliver them from what they deserve, and that they have to give up their centers to the church to have any hope of survival. What is more, they are told that God set it up this way, created this institution to function this way, and wants everyone to give their centers to it. To the extent that they absorb all these lessons, they are left with only one choice. As long as they do everything their religious institution tells them to do, they feel safe and secure, in the hands of a "good parent," God.

For some who grow up with the self-destructive core beliefs, the relationship that appears to hold the promise to fill the void, to heal all wounds, is the church.

The Rules behind Dysfunction

Codependent patterns of relating can also be learned in families that have no identifiable addiction, but operate by a rigid set of rules that precludes the development of wholesome individuality. Claudia Black, in *It Will Never Happen To Me*, sums up these stifling rules in three: don't talk, don't trust, don't feel. Robert Subby gives a more detailed list:

1. It's not okay to talk about problems.

2. Feelings should not be expressed openly.

3. Communication is best if indirect, with one person acting as messenger between two others (triangulation).

4. Unrealistic expectations — to be strong, good, right, perfect. Make us proud.

5. Don't be "selfish."

6. Do as I say, not as I do.

7. It's not okay to play or be playful.

8. Don't rock the boat.

9. Don't talk about sex.

(Lost in the Shuffle, 29)

The rules keep family members forever disconnected from each other, from anyone outside the family, and even from their inner selves. They live in isolation. Codependence is a very unhealthy but predictable response to this environment: a desperate attempt to bridge the isolation by "holding onto" someone.

1. *It's not okay to talk about problems.* The things we are most anxious about, or most fear, are the very ones no one is allowed to mention. Children are told: "Don't you worry about it; there's nothing wrong; everything is fine." Perhaps there is a family myth that attributes apparent trouble to some other "decoy" issue. Perhaps the "reassurance" carries with it a strong note of censure: "What a terrible thing to suggest that about Daddy. He works very hard for you." Whatever the ploy, the message is clear: don't bring up that subject again.

A book could be written about the Catholic hierarchy and this policy: it's not okay to talk about problems. The United States bishops had a meeting with the pope's representative. As the meeting opened, a timely letter from the pope stated what would not be discussed — clerical celibacy and the role of women — and those limits were observed. Priests met with their bishop to discuss problems close to their hearts — clergy morale and celibacy — and the meeting opened with the announcement that all discussion must remain "within the parameters of church teaching": thou shalt not question celibacy. The bishops will not challenge the pope and priests will not challenge the bishop for fear of "cutting off dialogue." What dialogue?

To the extent that church officials or members operate by these rules, they maintain and contribute to the overall state of dysfunction and to their own victimization.

A parochial school went into a state of crisis because of the don't-talk rule. The pastor had fired the principal. The teachers admired the principal and tried to question the decision, tried to talk about the problem. Did the pastor act alone? No one knew. What were the reasons? There was no statement. Even direct questions received no answer. The teachers asked that an independent arbitrator come in to facilitate open dialogue. Denied. An in-house "arbitrator" came from the diocese and started the "open dialogue" with these rules: only one teacher would be allowed to sit in on the discussion, and that teacher was forbidden to communicate any of the proceedings with her colleagues. The faculty resigned.

2. *Feelings should not be expressed openly.* "Nice people," Christian people, never get angry, or afraid, or resentful, or even really happy. It would be disloyal to the family to feel those things, and so they bury them until even they do not know they are there. "Children" of all ages in church families feel empty, burned out, lonely, angry at the system, but they have no forum, no permission to articulate those feelings. Their choices: anesthetize the feelings with religious mantras or rituals, numb them with sweets, valium, or scotch; block them with relentless busyness; or leave.

3. *Communication is best if indirect, with one person acting as messenger between two others (triangulation).* Spouses who will not speak to each other will send messages through the children. Or a mother may complain to one adult child about another one's behavior instead of confronting that son or daughter directly. The parties involved will not do the difficult work of facing each other's disagreement or discontent. The messenger is always stuck with the responsibility or making the relationship work, or making sure they understand each other.

Churches have mastered triangulation. The discontented will rarely approach their pastor with complaints. Instead they will discuss their grievances at great length with other church members. Members can leave a church over something the pastor said or did, and everyone else will know before the pastor.

Church groups seldom communicate with each other except through the pastor. The choir may assume they know how the women's club feels about an issue or are willing to accept the pastor's opinion of the club's point of view without sitting down with the club members themselves.

Some pastors and higher level prelates will deal with church members only through their secretary or staff. By the time the message gets through, if it does at all, the content has been filtered through one or several people, each an opinion on the relative worth of the message. So what the bishop hears from the people is limited to what the bishop's staff is willing to transmit. What the people hear from the bishop has been edited by a team of speech writers who compose what the people "should hear." Each side of the triangle is effectively insulated from the others. Without open communication, the system remains stuck.

4. *Unrealistic expectations — to be strong, good, right, perfect.* Make us proud. In this kind of family, one grade of B and the rest As, second string on the basketball team, third place out of fifty in the spelling bee, are all losers. Enough is never enough.

For some reason, "Be perfect as your heavenly Father is perfect" has been quoted in more sermons than "if your eye offends you, pluck it out," though it is no easier. If we listen well and are conscientious children, we can get on a ceaseless treadmill of "jobs for the Lord." I came to a point several years ago where I could not pray at all because my image of God had come to look like Uncle Sam on the recruiting poster, pointing his finger at me and saying, "Uncle Sam wants you."

In this kind of system, young seminarians can be made to feel they have only two choices: become a pastor or be a loser. Some "tough it out" because everyone outside of themselves is pushing them "upward," while everything inside of them wants to make another choice.

In this kind of church, we never say "burnout." We grab the first person who comes into church on Sunday, give her charge of the next fund-raiser, and do not let her off the hook until she resigns everything and tears up her membership card as well. Some church members have voluntarily taken on saving the church as their personal mission; they invest all their off-work hours in meetings and worry, often risking their families and their health. And then there are a few super-dedicated clerics who think they are going to change the church single-handedly by working fifteen-hour days, seven days a week — until the pressure catches up with them.

5. *Don't be "selfish."* This is particularly insidious because, if taken seriously, it robs the child of internal permission for any self-care. "Who are you thinking about right now? Yourself! Just yourself!" That is not wrong in and of itself; in fact, it is healthy to pursue one's interests, to want to enjoy some favorite dish, or to have a friend over. This accusation is more often a symptom of the parent's inability to cope, particularly if the parent is codependent and sees everyone else's wish as a command. The parent is clearly overwhelmed, and the child gets the message that he was bad for even asking.

Those programmed this way as children cannot, in adulthood, even wonder if their marriages might be abusive. The tape clicks on: "Who are you thinking about? Just yourself again? How about doing something to help? You should be grateful!" The choice is severely limited: be submissive or be "selfish."

Having personal needs is against the law in this system. Some "good Christians" have no inner sense of their own needs. The church has told them "what everyone needs," so if the pain increases, they just increase their dosage of the church prescription. If they still hurt, there must be something wrong with *them*. Those who do have a moment of awareness — that they need to take a break, or address some issues, or deal with anger or grief — either care for those needs in private or repress them.

6. *Do as I say, not as I do*. Members of some Christian denominations are caught in a bind: they cannot even wonder about their church's "official" teachings without having their loyalty questioned. They cannot talk about problems or feelings related to those teachings. They censor all intuition and thought, recognize only what is approved by the system, and repress all the rest. This inner split not only encourages members to give up their centers as a matter of misdirected piety, but, as Scott Peck pointed out in *People of the Lie*, creates people who "just follow orders" without question.

7. *It's not okay to play or be playful*. There is always more work to be done. Life is serious business. Life is a burden that one must carry alone. Besides, play is spontaneous, unpredictable, not under strict control, and we must not have that.

Liturgical celebrations in most of the mainline Christian denominations have lost any of the spontaneity that should characterize true celebration. Everything is so rigid and predictable that we neither open ourselves to one another, nor do we truly express our inner thankfulness. On the contrary, our liturgies sign and reinforce our isolation.

8. *Don't rock the boat*. Be quiet, don't make waves, go along with the program. In some churches, anyone who questions any policy is labeled disloyal. To take issue with internal injustices, to speak for the disenfranchised, or to suggest a more pro-active good-Samaritan policy is equated with challenging God.

Jesus was delivered over for public execution, and put to death, precisely for rocking the boat, making waves, and refusing to go along with the program. Jesus was not codependent. Yet in his name, we continue to support policies we know are wrong lest we rock the "bark of Peter." We refuse to take a more active stance on peace and justice issues lest we lose our "nice" white-gloves-on-Sunday image.

9. *Don't talk about sex.* We talk about it quite a lot, but communication is limited to repeating all the prohibitions. Church statements are often negative, fearful, even obsessive.

The churches that operate by Subby's rules isolate their members from outsiders, from one other, and from themselves. No one must ever talk to outsiders; anyone outside the "family" is "working for the devil." There is no room for discussion of problems among members of the "family"; some church officials even smile upon those "very loyal" followers who will report any questionable conversation. Personal thoughts and feelings, intuitions and initiatives must be handed over to the parent church. The church itself becomes the only point of connection allowed. One's bond with the church becomes as important as a young child's bond with parents: it is a matter of survival.

Codependence and Addiction

When children make choices to try to control their parent's erratic behavior or cut off their thoughts and feelings in order to conform, those children are adapting to survive. The environment is not healthy, but the tendency to adapt is a normal response. When these understandings and behaviors outlast childhood and become the established pattern in adult relationships, they no longer comprise a strategy necessary for survival, but have become codependence.

Codependents will "cut out their center" — that core of self that can think, feel, decide, and act — and hand that center over to someone else, either to another person, or to the family, or to some institution or system. The codependent then acts by "remote control," taking cues not from inside, but from that other source.

A person with a hole in the center is unstable. We cannot operate without a center, and so codependents will gravitate toward certain all-consuming relationships or toward mood-altering substances or activities that will take over the functions of the lost center — to fill the void with meaning, value, purpose, and a sense of direction. They will typically cling to this substitute-center even when the thoughts, feelings, and actions it dictates begin to destroy their lives. They will hold on as if survival depended on it, as if they had no other choice.

A decade ago it was thought that codependence was "caught" by living with an addict, but now it is recognized that it is the *pre-existent* condition of inner emptiness — codependence — that drives individuals into unhealthy relationships. Codependents will actually choose as life-partners individuals who have the potential for creating the same dysfunction they experienced at home: it feels right.

These relationships can become so unbearable that the codependent may look for relief from this pain in other substances or processes. Codependents are "set up" for addictions. In fact, codependence itself fits the definition of addiction: "the out of control and aimless searching for wholeness, happiness, and peace through . . . a pathological love and trust relationship with an object or event" (Nakken, *The Addictive Personality: Roots, Rituals and Recovery,* 4–10).

The Codependent Roles and Patterns in the Family

Codependence describes a number of roles whose common denominator is reactivity to others outside oneself. Enablers, heroes, scapegoats, lost children, and mascots all take their cues from another person or from their church or family system. These compensatory roles, first identified by Sharon Wegscheider-Cruse, are caricatures — extremes — of healthy functioning. They are roles that become compulsive responses to problems and train the child to become a codependent adult.

The "prime enabler" is usually the spouse of the acting-out person, who covers for that person and works overtime to convince the children, the neighbors, and her- or himself that "we're all fine." This is all well-intentioned; in fact, I think most of us were trained to do this. The enabler tries to make life easier for the addict so that "stress" doesn't get the better of him or her, tries to keep the children quiet and "perfect" to prevent "stress" and another round of addictive behavior, and tries to keep up the family image.

Enabling roles may be easy to spot in a church whose pastor is actively addicted to alcohol or some other substance or process, or in a religious community whose superior is an active addict. The members of that parish or community will tend to ignore, "not see," downplay, rationalize, or compensate for the pastor's or superior's behavior. Perhaps the housekeeper or secretary will make excuses while the pastor is "sleeping it off." Members may be overfunctioning to cover the pastor's responsibilities. A woman from Minnesota once told me what a difficult time they were having getting used to their new nonaddicted pastor.

They had worked around an alcoholic pastor for so long that they were better at getting things done by playing their dysfunctional roles and avoiding each other than they were at open and honest communication with each other and with the pastor.

Enablers deny the seriousness of the problem to protect the dream of what this family or church could be. As time goes on, though, the dream becomes more wish than reality, and even a glimpse of the truth is very painful. They have to continually block what they know and feel in order to hold onto the happy ideal, or hope that the problem will somehow just go away. This does violence to the inner self, but the alternative seems too horrible to face. And so the enablers will continue in their monumental efforts and considerable denial until they "hit bottom."

At the same time, the enablers try to protect the children — or the other members of the church — from this inner torment by refusing to discuss their own fears and by dismissing the fears of others as foolish or unfounded. So real problems are never discussed or even mentioned. Based on the false hope that no one else has noticed, this strategy keeps everyone locked up in separate cells with "the secret," while the addicts or pivotal persons never have to face any of the painful consequences of their damaging behavior.

Enablers operate from the assumption that if they do all the right things, they can control, change, or hide the behavior of another person in any circumstances, and particularly when that person is acting out the addiction or compulsion. The task is impossible, the efforts futile, but the enablers continue because they are afraid to stop and may actually feel unable to stop. Such persons have become as addicted to the addicts and to their own codependent role as the addict is to his or her drug of choice. To sustain the relationship, to "save" the spouse or the children, to "save" the pastor or the bishop or the church, *enablers will even sacrifice personal self-worth and the very moral values they are so determined to protect.*

The enabler teaches the children, by word and example, to center their lives around the addicted, compulsive, or emotionally absent person. The children act out their other-centeredness in one or more recognizable roles. One of the children, frequently the eldest, plays the family hero: the picture of success in school but inwardly insecure, feeling responsible for making the parent happy so he won't withdraw, won't have to drink or act out. Another child is the scapegoat, always in trouble, someone whom the family can blame for their pain. The lost child is the quiet one; she provides relief — we never have to worry about her — but develops little sense of self or emotion. And then there's the mascot, the clown, who uses humor and other means to distract attention from the problem.

Each of these learns to do whatever the current state of crisis needs or allows; they take their cues from the mood of the addicted, compulsive, or distant person or from the needs of the system. When things are looking bad, they perform their roles in the drama. The hero will take an after-school job or do three extra book reports. The lost child will disappear. The mascot is a noticeable gauge of the family stress level: the more distressing the situation, the more foolish and distracting his behavior. The scapegoat will inevitably cause some trouble; this child is the family's cry for help. At very least, mom and dad will have to talk to each other *about him*; at best, some authority will prescribe family counseling.

In religious communities where the superior is an active addict, one of the sisters may take on the hero role by writing a book to bring honor on the convent. One of the brothers in the order may become a "problem" that gives everyone something to worry about and on whom they can blame their emotional unrest. In churches with an addicted pastor, the president of the parish council may be very entertaining and glibly distract from the pastor's tardiness with a few amusing anecdotes. In fact, the whole parish council can be the parish mascot: they can arrange a social event grand enough that it will keep everyone compulsively busy for months and distract them from the sick pastor and their own inability to deal openly and honestly with each other. Many, many members of local churches qualify as "lost children": they disappear into their homes and never say a word, even if they disagree with or have been hurt by the prevailing dysfunction.

In each of these cases, we may be looking at the compensatory behavior of various group members — easily identifiable examples of codependence — but those persons are manifesting the pain of entire groups. Groups as a whole exhibit their codependence in subtler ways — cooperating in the denial of the problem and enabling the problem to continue. The chemical dependence of the leaders depicted is only one type of addiction; there are others, more subtle, more difficult to identify and avoid. Church families can be dysfunctional in all the ways household families can be.

Behind the Roles

No matter how well they play their roles, the children of dysfunctional families — and members of dysfunctional churches — cannot stop the problem, any more than they can stop the tide with their sand pails, yet there is a drive to repeat the behavior in the desperate hope that this time it will work. Just like their parents, the children are doing what does not work and doing it over and over because they are afraid to stop. The entire family system is involved in codependent or addictive behavior.

The system seems to "need" someone to blame, someone to pin hopes on, someone to provide comic relief, in order to maintain its unhealthy balance. The hero may fall from grace and become the scapegoat; one person can play two roles at once. When there are vacancies, family members will slide right into those roles because they have been trained to react to cues outside themselves, cues from the family, instead of listening to their own inner sense of who they are.

Many members of the clergy, many holders of special religious roles, are the family heroes of their own dysfunctional families of origin: that is why they sought a career in church. Such individuals came to their church roles already trained from youth to react, to compensate for dysfunction, and to look good rather than do anything that might "upset" mom or dad.

We learn as children an unhealthy set of rules and assumptions that cripple us as adults and sabotage our relationships. The same is true in church. For centuries we were a church of children, accepting that we were no good and doing what we needed to do to survive. We are just beginning to face our church codependence now because certain things we had taken for granted have begun to fall apart. In the last few decades, as we have begun to take more adult responsibilities, we have found very quickly how blind we are to the presence of God and the good in ourselves and others, how crippled we are in our abilities to make decisions and act, how "stuck" the whole church family is because of our collective codependence.

Some Churches, Some Members, More Than Others

Some churches are more codependent than others; it is a matter of degree. To the extent that any church — whether local community or international body — values persons without centers over healthy individuals, or rewards reactive behavior but punishes responsible action, it is dysfunctional and teaches codependence. To the extent that a church assigns its members roles to play and expects them to live by rules that rob them of their inner selves, it is dysfunctional and teaches codependence. To the extent that a church is a closed system, it is dysfunctional and teaches codependence.

Also, within any church, some individuals have been more harmed by this than others, depending on the messages they received about their own worth and the role of the church from their families, depending on the particular church communities in which they were raised and the attitudes that prevailed throughout their education. So while some church members may be severely handicapped by codependence, others may be affected relatively little. While some may be nearly blind to the good in themselves and others, to the presence of God beyond the walls of their institution, others may experience only a little clouding of vision once in a while.

2

Shame, Abandonment, Abuse

There are two other elements — shame and abandonment — that can help deepen our understanding of the causes and contributing factors of codependence. Shame is an internal sense that something is inherently wrong with oneself. Shame is not the same as guilt, or regret, for some wrong act. It is deeper, more pervasive. Guilt may admit, "I made a mistake"; shame says, "I *am* a mistake." Shame helps to burn the hole in our centers, the hole that we later try to fill with codependent relationships or addictions.

Childhood experiences of abandonment and abuse can drive people into a deep sense of shame, can create a hole in their center, the black hole of codependence.

Abandonment does not necessarily mean actual physical separation, though that is one possible type of abandonment. If a parent has died, divorced, been away for extended periods of time, children will frequently blame themselves for the absence. "If I were good, Dad would not have gone away."

Abandonment can also include emotional distance, family enmeshment, or using the child to meet the parents' emotional needs. Emotional distance is caused by the failure of the parent or significant adult to mirror back to the child who that child is, to validate the child's feelings, to provide a secure place where the child can safely be dependent. In such a case, the child experiences abandonment and concludes that Mom and Dad either do not like those feelings or place no importance on them, so the feelings must be bad. Feeling anything then becomes an occasion that triggers shame.

Enmeshment is the absorption of the child's individuality into the giant family identity: behavior, opinions, even extracurricular interests are all prescribed to fit the image of The Family. It is hard to tell where any one member begins or ends. It may look more like smothering than abandonment, but the truth is that the child inside, who is a unique individual, who needs to be cherished and affirmed, has been ignored, neglected, abandoned, or lost.

Abandonment can also occur when adults attempt to parent while they still have an empty hole in the center of themselves that they're trying to fill. They are very likely in codependent relationships with their partners, possibly in addictive patterns with other substances or processes. They deny, minimalize, or simply do not see their child's needs, and use their child to fill their own needs for loving presence, validation, security, and comfort. Using children this way is a form of abandonment of those children: there is no *parent* there for them.

Such children often cannot even recognize their own needs — emotional needs or normal dependency needs — because those needs put them in conflict with the parent. Who will care for whom? "Perfect" children, it seems, should have no needs. So they learn to repress their own needs — to consider them something to be hidden, something bad, a source of shame.

Abandonment may be compounded by abuse: the child feels isolated from the parent, and the isolation is maintained by some form of emotional, physical, or sexual cruelty.

Children who are victims of abuse feel hurt, afraid, helpless, empty, and alone. On some level, they feel humiliation and rage, though they may not "get in touch with" those feelings until midlife or later. In fact, the more severe the abandonment or abuse, the more the child may tend to idealize the family. In the child's eyes, the parent is God and can do no wrong. Besides, the child is so totally dependent on the parents and unable to risk losing them, that none of these feelings can safely be expressed. The conclusion that children draw from abuse is that they must be very bad and must deserve that kind of abuse just for being who they are.

The cycle of abuse, abandonment, and shame is multi-generational and self-perpetuating. These children's bodies grow up to be adult bodies. They have learned that the way to be accepted, in even a limited way, is to be capable, to repress their own needs and take care of all the needs of the parent or significant other, to become indispensable to that other person. But inside the adult body with the caretaker role lives that little child, abandoned long ago, afraid to have needs or to make them known for fear that they will be abandoned again.

Because of their shame, they cannot admit to those needs openly or seek healthy means to fill them. They end up hoping that their spouses or their children will love them unconditionally and fill their needs as their parents should have done. So these second-generation young children cannot acknowledge their own needs and feel instead the obligation to take care of their parents.

The "hole" is thus handed on to another generation. People with holes where their centers should be seek to fill those holes with mood-altering substances, processes, or codependent relationships.

A system that abandons its children, abuses and shames them, produces children that are high risk for becoming codependent or addicted. Whether that system is the Jones family or the Catholic church, the process is the same. Shame, abandonment, and abuse rob members of their centers, their ability to feel what they feel, to know what they know, to make choices and take responsibilities as whole persons. Shame, abandonment, and abuse create codependent Christians.

Original Sin

That drama of shame, abandonment, and abuse also plays itself out in the church family.

From the time most of us were very young, we heard the story of "the original sin." It says that humankind started in a garden of perfect harmony with God and nature, but that the first man created to live there disobeyed God. Since then and because of him, all humans are born wretched sinners, carrying the guilt of that first sin and in a state of utter alienation from God.

God, in perfect justice, demanded that this act of disobedience against the Perfect Parent be punished with abandonment, death, and childbirth pain. And, since we all share the guilt, we all deserve to die. But instead of all humans facing death, God assigned the one whom God cared for the most, Jesus, to die a torturous death alone. He took our punishment on himself.

Some Christians today describe "original sin" as a collective influence to which we all contribute and find the notion valuable in articulating their personal experience of sin and alienation. It is difficult to integrate a deeper sense of sin — both personal and collective — and a more compassionate understanding of God with the literal meaning of the old story. It is time to take a second look at that.

Contemporary writings have suggested that the Garden of Eden may be a projection of human longing for a state of perfect harmony with God and the universe, a state that we long for and seem unable to attain. Some say that perhaps the only unity of life that humans have experienced happened in the womb and not in a garden.

Some exegetes suggest that the eating of the fruit symbolizes human sin and demonstrates that sin destroys harmony and causes alienation. The story of "Adam" or "Everyman" is, according to these scholars, a prototype of, but not the cause of, subsequent human actions.

The tenet that depravity and total alienation from God are part of the human condition is not found in Genesis. It is possible that the understanding of human nature we have been conditioned to accept may, like the garden, be a projection of our own human experiences of being parented. Those who have known shame and abandonment may have projected them onto all human children and the Divine Parent.

The teaching on original sin that many of us heard as children said we were born in shame. As we learned the stories that are the core of our Christian tradition, we learned to accept that shame and to define our relationship with God in those terms. We learned that there was something about us — the mark of our ancestor's sin — that made us repulsive in God's eyes from the time we were born.

God is described in this story as a terribly exacting, even cruel, parent who decided that death is the appropriate penalty for disobedience. And not only did our ancestors receive that sentence, but all of humankind is guilty by association. We were told that we all deserve to be abandoned by our ultimate parent, God, and that we deserve to die.

We learned the conditions for escaping our fate. Jesus took our place, but — in Catholic theology, at least — we are not automatically covered by this heroic act of substitution. Though Jesus' suffering and death paid the supreme price for us, it is the church alone who can dispense the merits of Christ, can stay the condemning hand of God. We were taught that we are entirely dependent on the institutional church. Our relationship with church, then, was built on fear and on the belief that only the church could save us from being abandoned for all eternity to the pits of hell.

A relationship that is shame-based and built on fear of abandonment is necessarily going to be addictive or codependent. If we cling to the church because of our sense of shame or because we are convinced that we must remain dependent on that church or be totally abandoned, then in our minds the church holds the power to give us worth, to make us whole, to give us the love Mom and Dad did not, to fill the hole in our centers. If we are totally dependent, we have no room to question, no room for feelings, no permission to trust anyone beyond the system.

It is very difficult for us to hear this line of thinking; it sounds abusive on someone's part. We have a ready answer: the Creator *had to* think and act as our teachers described. The Divine Parent had to reject us, had to require the ultimate penalty for disobedience against the ultimate authority. God did it because it was the only right thing to do, and God did it for our own good (the "logic" of an abusive parent). Furthermore, our teachers *had to* be right; that is guaranteed. The church is never wrong; God promised us that. It is a closed circle, and there is only one answer inside.

The Genesis story originated as a piece of Hebrew folklore, a story that told of the relationship of the Jewish people with God. The Jewish people do not and have not considered this story a lesson about inherited sin or guilt as Christians do. It is a story of human alienation from God — typical of, but not the cause of, each one's alienation from God and others. It appears in a series of other stories that tell of other alienations — brother from brother, shepherd from farmer, tribe from tribe, culture from culture. We make the wrong choices, we sin, we separate ourselves from that special garden of intimacy, and yet God continues to offer us hope and love. From this understanding, one can draw very different conclusions about our relationship with God.

Jesus did not teach original sin. He did not rail on the depravity of the human race. He did not preach inherent sinfulness or doom. As God's representative, he certainly did not embody the harsh and judging God we picture setting the death sentence. Jesus taught a gentle acceptance for the weakness of those who stumbled along, who tried to do the right thing but often missed the mark. The ones he really took to task were those who hid their own shame behind religious authority and tried to shame others. Jesus' parables are full of God's open-armed, loving acceptance, not of shame and abandonment.

Poisonous Pedagogy

The pattern of parenting based on the idea that obedience is the ultimate virtue, that disobedience is the worst sin, and that parents are required in justice to chastise all spontaneity, independence, and self-esteem in their children, is what German psychologist Alice Miller, in her book *For Your Own Good*, labels "poisonous pedagogy." Children raised according to this "spare the rod, spoil the child" method, retain buried feelings of humiliation and rage, but consciously idealize their parents, insisting that what was done to them was done for their own good. Both the conscious acceptance of those rules and the unconscious need to vent those buried emotions on someone else contribute to their adult choices to repeat the cycle of shaming and abuse.

Looking at our church fathers from a family-systems perspective reveals evidence that points to the conclusion that the Christian retelling of the Genesis story, with an emphasis on sin as the basis of our relationship with God and an insistence on death as the just penalty for disobedience, projects onto God the distorted image of the ideal parent that was learned in their human families (Augustine's story follows in chapter 3).

Many generations of Christians who have lived since those early theologians have been all too ready to accept that version of the story because it correlates with their own experiences of authority and parental behavior.

Among the principles of poisonous pedagogy that Alice Miller lists are these: all adults deserve respect and obedience; children never deserve respect; a feeling of duty produces love; tenderness, self-esteem, and responding to a child's needs are all harmful; obedience, severity, and coldness are good preparation for life (*For Your Own Good*, 59, 60). Many adults will recognize this pattern in the "good Christian training" they received as children. Miller points out that those who carried out the orders of the Third Reich came from good Catholic and Lutheran homes. They were taught that "all authority comes from God," without being allowed to distinguish between true godly authority and abuse.

Miller traces the connections between childhood experiences of poisonous pedagogy and the feelings it brings about, and the behavior and motivations of the same people when they become adults. She uses the examples of known criminals and leaders of Nazi Germany and demonstrates how their crimes were reenactments of the kinds of abuse that they received as children. She describes the process by which one learns to idealize the abuser, adopt the abuser's motives, and continue the pattern:

1. The child is hurt without anyone recognizing the situation as hurtful.

2. The child fails to react to the resulting suffering with anger.

3. The child must show gratitude for what are supposed to be good intentions.

4. The child forgets/blocks everything.

5. The child-become-adult discharges the stored-up anger onto others or directs it against himself. (*For Your Own Good*, 106)

Both the content and the tone of some of our church teaching, particularly on sin, sex, and power, still continue this cycle.

The Medieval Church

Though there were individuals in the Middle Ages who understood the God-human relationship in a different light, popular attention was drawn to the guilt of humanity and the punishment deserved as a result of sin. The average church-goer had no education, was taught in church (by priests who often had little education themselves) about a God as distant and powerful as the pope or the emperor. They received the impression that the "kingdom of God" paralleled feudal society: they were born serfs and sinners, rejected by God. And they lived in dread of an eternity of "well-deserved" torture after death.

The leaders of the institutional church, on the other hand, distanced themselves from that shame. They claimed to have the power to apply the "treasury of the church," the "merits of Christ and the saints," to cover some or all of the punishment owed because of sin and thereby to connect peasants to their Creator. They charged gold coins for one of these treasury notes — certificates of indulgence they were called — and the peasants were so helpless and so shamed, and saw the church as so powerful and "shameless," that they did scrape together what money they could to ransom the souls of their departed loved ones from suffering.

The medieval Christian's sense of utter worthlessness and dependence on the power of the institutional church for any value is recognized today as codependence. Medieval Christians had holes where their centers should have been, nothing about them was good, and they needed something or someone else to fill those holes and give them worth.

Confessing one's sins to a priest was absolutely necessary. And beyond that, one still had to make up for the punishment due those sins. Masses, sacraments, pilgrimages to shrines, visits to relics of dead saints, even fighting in Crusades and killing nonbelievers, all entitled participants to units of this church treasury.

If one could amass enough merit points to out-tally the punishment-due-to-sin points, one might have a chance to prevent or shorten abandonment after death. But they had to keep earning, confessing, and earning some more to remain ahead of their spiritual debt. This led to religious compulsion, to codependence in their relationship with church.

It is hard enough for someone today to step out of codependence once it is recognized, but to the naive church member of the Middle Ages, this codependence had "God's own" endorsement.

The codependence of the people — fear of God and death, the buying of indulgences, compulsive scrupulosity — and the shame-less power of the institution, brought European Christianity to a point of crisis.

Martin Luther

Martin Luther grew up in this atmosphere of poisonous pedagogy. His father was strict and demanding. The God of his youth was made in the image of his father and of the church. He found himself in deep shame and plagued with that sense of guilt that was sanctioned by his own father and his super-parent, the church.

Luther became an Augustinian monk. He identified with the wide gulf between God and humankind that the church was preaching because he had similar childhood experiences; he was plagued with the same feelings of shame and was ready to condemn every human inclination as evil.

Compulsive scrupulosity became his response: he fretted over being meticulous enough in his examination of conscience to make a *perfect* accounting of sins. He believed what the church told him: that he had to be exact in confessing the nature and number of every sin, or else God would not forgive him.

Luther "hit bottom" when the impossibility of being perfectly accurate drove him to near despair. A professor of New Testament studies at the University of Wittenberg, he searched the Scriptures for a solution.

The way out of the dilemma was letting go of the scrupulosity, letting go of the compulsion to earn salvation, and simply trusting that, if he put his faith in God, God would forgive him and welcome him as a son. He no longer needed to depend on a compulsive use of the rites of the church, but could approach God directly. The way out of his compulsive activity was to recognize that he had no power to control those things, that God does care about him, and that God is not controlled by the church. He put his faith in God and trusted God to accept him and take away his sin.

Today we call those attitudinal changes the first, second, and third steps of the Twelve Step program. They lead to healthy recovery from addictive behavior.

Luther found the way to recovery, a way out of church codependence, and was courageous in leading the way for others. But he was not able to re-imagine the parenthood of God or any other God-and-human family context than the kind he had experienced with his father or learned from his church. When Luther taught about God, he repeated the lessons about the abject sinfulness of humans and the distant generosity of God that had fed his codependence and compulsivity in the first place.

Preaching Codependence

Some of our most influential Christian thinkers were shame-based, abandoned, and abused. Their shame comes first and defines them; God's love responds and rescues them. God is above and beyond them, distant and perfect; they are intrinsically flawed, utterly rejectable. Their sense of God is the necessary counterbalance to their own experience of wretchedness. The proof of the greatness of God's love is the forgiveness and eventual acceptance of creatures so despicable. One cannot accept the common approach to spirituality without accepting both extremes.

The experience of abuse scars children, leaves them unable to articulate what happened but able only to act it out. For generations we have been unable to say that we fear the angry "God who killed Jesus," but we behave compulsively to remain on good terms with this "God who loves us." We deny that the church has employed the methods of poisonous pedagogy; yet we employ the same methods with our students or church members and still cannot speak for ourselves in the face of "power." We cannot question — often cannot even *see* what is happening — and so we repeat the same unhealthy pattern and program our children with more fear of abandonment, because, after all, it was done to us for our own good.

The common, sin-based, shame-based spirituality is not the same as Jesus' approach. Jesus' actions do not operate out of the mindset of inherent sinfulness and deserved abandonment. God's parental love was his starting point. He had supper at the houses of sinners, gently easing them back from their errors.

Jesus did not convey the attitude that every human inclination was befouled with sin, just that people sometimes lose the way. He did not portray the attitude of ready rejection that the religious leaders projected onto God. On the other hand, he did deliver stern warnings to the self-righteous, to those religious leaders by whose religious perfectionism many stood condemned.

The gospel of codependence is a subtle form of poisonous pedagogy, a theology based on shame and fear of abandonment. The gospel of codependence is a theology that seems rational on one level but is abusive on another level; church members often experience emotional distancing, family enmeshment, and an obligation to affirm and protect (to "parent") their religious "parents." It has replaced the simple gospel of the person we claim to follow. Jesus' life and teaching affirmed and empowered ordinary persons; our theology based on shame still claims excessive power for a few ecclesiastical "adults" and reduces all others to the status of children in a system where children have no rights.

Part II

Sexual Abuse in the Church Family

3

The Family Secret

It is coming to light that sexual abuse is more common than we would like to believe. Both physical sexual abuse, and the more subtle forms of emotional sexual abuse, cause children to be crippled in later adult relationships. The shame is so deep, and the need to deny or escape so strong, that many who were sexually abused, either physically or emotionally, as children have no conscious memories of the incidents until middle age.

Just as sexual abuse is a hidden problem in a number of dysfunctional families, it is also one of the quieter factors in our dysfunction as church. Many of us have a deep distrust of our own sexuality and can attribute that in large part to the teachings and the attitudes of our churches. While all churches are presently trying to come to a more balanced view, the old messages and feelings we learned to associate with sex remain at the core of our church codependence.

In some churches, sex is not only not mentioned, but unmentionable. Members are living out, at least in their public lives, a rejection of sexuality, living the illusion that the waters of baptism put out all fires.

Other religious groups are almost obsessively preoccupied with their own taboos about sex. Questions of sexual morality rate more attention — *much* more — than the issues of social justice and nuclear suicide. It has become the constant theme of their preaching and writing.

Skeletons in the Closet

Augustine is an example of the relationship between family systems and theology. He was a prominent theologian who lived in the late fourth

41

and early fifth centuries and remains the single most influential Christian writer on sexual morality. Augustine told his parents' story and his own in his *Confessions.*

Augustine's mother, Monica, was the victim of a very rigid upbringing, what Alice Miller would call "poisonous pedagogy." Her parents had entrusted her care to a maidservant, whose disciplinary style was austere. She was determined to "break" the children of even their natural desires so that they would be able to resist greater temptations later in life. All day long, when little Monica was "parched and dry," she was forbidden even a sip of water. The point of this extreme measure was the development of "self-discipline," so that when Monica reached maturity and was mistress of the house, she would not be tempted by the contents of the wine cellar, but could "control her thirst" against even the most adverse temptation.

With what we know now of addictions, one has to wonder about that maidservant. Was she herself a compulsive drinker, trying to spare her young charge the same agony? Was she the wife or daughter of an alcoholic, trying to control another generation as she wished she had been able to control her elders? In either case, she succeeded — not in passing on control — but in passing on her own obsession.

Augustine goes on to say that Monica did fall prey to the lure of the wine cellar. While still a girl, when her parents sent her down to the cellar to refill the pitcher from the dinner table, she "moistened her lips just a bit" with the wine before filling the pitcher. Gradually she increased her taste to a sip, and the sip to a cup. Finally, the same ever-vigilant maidservant confronted Monica about the drinking and drove the message home with insults. Monica was so stung by the verbal abuse that she immediately stopped sneaking drinks in the cellar.

Later in life, however, as Augustine noted, Monica made it a practice to carry with her a basket of fine foods and wine to share with others. She kept a cup of wine in hand *at all times* — diluted wine, of course, for she was a proper lady — from which she sipped frequently and which she always offered to share with others.

Monica reached adulthood abusively disciplined and shamed into docile submission. She used alcohol daily, all day. And she was trained to be codependent.

Monica was given in marriage to Patricius, a hard-working, ambitious man who was given to sleeping with other women and venting his violent temper at home. Monica handled this situation by applying what she had learned — perfect submission and self-effacement. She said she regarded the marriage vows as a declaration of her servanthood. From that time on, she guarded everything she said, never challenging her husband on anything. She advised other women to follow her practice of virtuous passivity, going so far as to say that if they were beaten it was because they were not careful enough.

Above all, Monica prayed for her husband. She prayed that he would convert to Christianity so that he would become chaste and remain faithful to her. Her hopes were that the church would make him change, that it would take away all his compulsive behavior and her pain.

Monica may have been married to a sexual addict; the rages are typical of addictive behavior. She responded in classic codependent style. Taking responsibility for his anger, trying to control it by giving up more and more of herself, and priding herself on being able to "hold it all together" in such adverse circumstances — all are diagnostic criteria of codependence (Timmen L. Cermak, *Diagnosing and Treating Co-dependence*, 11).

Now, with a sense of the family context, we can turn our attention to Augustine himself. Young Augustine was bright and quick, alive with a variety of interests, including a love of sports. His father made sacrifices so that he could have an education, first in his home city of Tagaste, and later in Carthage. But in school, any time he exhibited an interest in anything other than studies, he was given a beating by his tutor. He used to pray to the Christian God, the God his mother worshipped, to bring an end to the beatings. He felt that God could have intervened, but God never did stop them. His mother, the one parent he knew loved him, laughed aloud at his fear — he was just a foolish child who did not know what was good for him.

He learned the lesson of the prescribed schoolroom beatings and rose to the role of the hero, doing well in his studies, excelling in literature and oratory.

At the same time, his social behaviors more typified the family scapegoat: he was irresponsible and promiscuous. He and some friends shook all the fruit out of a neighbor's pear tree, just for the thrill of the moment. Girls were there for the taking, too. His mother admonished him to leave other men's wives alone; he admits that he ignored all of her warnings.

In his early twenties, he took one long-term mistress. He brought her with him when he moved to Italy in search of better teaching jobs. The relationship did not become a partnership of whole persons who could challenge each other's ideas and share each other's dreams. Augustine fathered a son with his mistress, but he developed his mind and sharpened his wit in the company of other men.

Augustine began to climb the career ladder. The city fathers of Milan sought his services as tutor to their sons. He reached a point where the next logical step, as he saw it, would be a politically well-connected marriage. His mother, too, had been encouraging marriage so that, thus "restrained" by the marriage commitment, he could be baptized and forgiven of all he had done before. (A true and ever hopeful codependent, it never occurred to her that marriage never stopped his father.)

A friend and companion in studies tried to convince Augustine not to marry, voicing concern that, once married, he would not be as free to pursue the intellectual pleasures they enjoyed together. Augustine assured him that he would continue to make time for those, but that he could not live without satisfying his sexual passions.

His mistress was a liability to these new career ambitions, so he sent her — the woman he had lived with for ten years — back to North Africa, kept his son, and proposed marriage to the daughter of a powerful man. He received permission to marry the girl, provided he wait two years for her to come of age. He admitted that it upset him greatly to send his mistress away, and so, since marriage would be two whole years away, he took an interim mistress to keep him company while he waited for his bride.

The picture of Augustine's first thirty years is not virtue by the usual standard. From a twentieth-century perspective, Augustine was addicted to sex. He knowingly made destructive choices just for the thrill and the danger involved — from destroying an orchard to bedding the wives of Tagaste — a tendency typical of sexual addiction.

He was parented by a sexually compulsive and raging man and a confirmed codependent who may also have been alcoholic. That had to have colored his view of the world. He was accustomed to self-effacing, codependent women and men who indulged every inclination.

It does not seem that Augustine experienced real friendships with women as he did with men. Perhaps that is because women of his time had no opportunity for education or because he chose to associate with women who were not his intellectual equal and was therefore not able to see them as partners. Perhaps he chose less intelligent women because he believed that women *could not* be equals. In any event, the experiences he chose and the beliefs he held served to reinforce each other.

His idea of commitment was staying with the one mistress for as long as he did. It included the right to send her away when her services were no longer needed.

In Augustine's experience, sex was not an expression of committed love and deepening relationship; sex was a need, a drive, a hunger. He used women to satisfy that hunger.

The Split between Belief and Practice

Perhaps one of the most damaging traits was Augustine's ability to separate his behavior from his belief system. As a child, he was a victim of abuse and emotional abandonment. He experienced rages from his father, beatings from his teacher, and emotional abandonment by his mother. He was shamed and a victim of poisonous pedagogy, and these experiences colored his theology.

He bore the marks of a destructive upbringing but could not question the appropriateness of his beatings because all the generations before him had gone through the same course of study with the same punishments and deemed it best for him, because his mother condoned them and he considered his mother a saint, and because, in his mind, God sanctioned the beatings by allowing them to continue.

As do many abused children, he had to "live in two minds" from the time he was very young because the message of his parents' love and teacher's care, which he so wanted to believe, was irreconcilable with the reality of the abuse.

He questioned the beatings only briefly. In the end, he accepted the message of the disciplinary code: *he* was bad, and the system — backed by history, Mom, and God — was right. To do that, he had to deny the knowledge and feelings of his own experience and accept the contrary set of rights and wrongs that he was taught. He could not know what he knew, or feel what he felt — those thoughts and feelings were now sources of shame. That left a hole in his center: a disdain for self, a sense of shame before others, and a driving need to fill the void. What he allowed himself to know — what he could view as "right" — had to come from outside.

Gnosticism was the prevalent philosophy of life at that time: belief that the world was divided into two realms, good and evil, light and darkness. The good consisted of things intellectual, spiritual, not of this world. Everything else, everything physical or material, was inherently evil. The human person was a mind-spirit caught in, and trying to escape from, a body.

It is difficult for some of us today to imagine a whole culture going along with this philosophy. But the ascetic life can be generally accepted as a value without it being commonly practiced as a way of life. That was evidently true in the fourth-century Roman world, it was certainly the case in the Catholic church when I was growing up, and it is still held true among a smaller segment of the Catholic population today. I know people who think that the married life runs a poor second to celibacy in terms of life-value and holiness, even if they can't live by those standards themselves. They feel they are the less because they "just don't have what it takes" to "do the higher and holier thing."

During the period when he was living with his mistress, Augustine was a member of the Manichees, a gnostic sect that espoused asceticism and abstinence as the ideal lifestyle. During those years, Augustine was *saying* he believed in the superiority of sexual abstinence, but was never able to live it. His choices violated his own values; he was "living in two minds," in a situation of inner conflict that must have carried some personal dissatisfaction.

Conversion to Celibacy

Two factors brought about Augustine's moment of conversion. One was the intellectual search for answers, the other was an escape from inner emptiness and the sexual compulsion he used to fill it.

During this period, he became aware of communities of celibate men living in the desert in North Africa. This must have looked like gnostic heaven: an invitation to cast off everything — career and women — and seek God dwelling in unapproachable light. Conversion to Christianity was, in that sense, one more step in the same direction as his Manichaeism.

In addiction circles, a big distinction is made between abstinence, which is doing without the substance or process, and true sobriety or recovery. One can refrain from using the addictive substance or process without ever having dealt with the inner beliefs and attitudes that motivate the need. Such a person is sometimes called a "dry drunk" because he or she is displaying the same negativity and craziness as before, but without the chemical. To live in true sobriety requires participation in a recovery program that will help one replace old destructive attitudes and behaviors with another, healthier set of beliefs.

Augustine was an abstinent, but *not recovering*, sex addict. His theology betrays the obsession of an addict.

According to Augustine, the first human couple, living in paradise, approached intercourse with as much passion as I can muster for mopping the floor: doing what needs to be done to maintain life. It was a purely intellectual choice and act, both carried out without any intrusion of nasty passion.

God did not create desire; passion came about only because of sin.

Augustine bemoaned the fact that after the sin and the advent of concupiscence, intercourse was no longer a purely intellectual choice for the continuation of the species. Passion was not only leading the way, but had even become a necessary part of the act: further evidence of the moral decay of humankind!

According to Augustine, sexual intercourse is almost always a sin, and a sin of such magnitude as to totally cut off one's relationship with God. The only conditions he could see for intercourse within marriage without serious sin were these: focused intent to procreate, concentration only on creating new little Christians, with *no pleasure* and no mental consent to any pleasure. By extension of that principle, it might be possible for one partner to remain passive and, therefore, sinless, to accommodate the passion of the other partner to save him or her from adultery. Inorgasmia was truly a virtue; enjoyment was a sin.

He was open about his intent, too: he wanted it all to end! The prescribed tests of will power would be so difficult that couples would simply cease all sexual intercourse, which would bring about an end of the human world and all its ugly desire and would herald the beginning of completely "spiritual" living in heaven. Taken all together, Augustine's ideas about sex sound like the ravings of a "dry drunk."

Augustine did write some lovely thoughts on the meaning of marriage, commentaries on Ephesians 5, explaining the scriptural assertion that marriage is a sign of Christ's union with the church. But since, in his own life, passion was always a source of shame, he could never reconcile this symbolic holiness with the reality of human passion. While he could admit a kind of theological parallel between Jesus' union of human and divine natures and the marriage union of male and female, he thought that that symbolic holiness would be corrupted as soon as the couple gave in to concupiscence.

From "Dry Drunk" to Church Policy

Augustine was not alone among the writers of his time to take this view of sex. He was a moderate among Gnostics, avoiding the extremes of asceticism and license; but seen through today's eyes, his was a grim moderation. There were others of his contemporaries who were equally negative. Clerical celibacy was first suggested in the fourth century. Negative attitudes toward sex were common in that period.

What distinguishes Augustine from the others is the sheer volume and wide influence of his writing. He wrote more on sex and marriage than any other Christian theologian up to that point. His writings have provided the source material for nearly all theological discussions of the topics of sex and marriage until the present time and the basis for church policies on birth control and mandatory celibacy.

That Augustine lived a wanton life before his conversion was never a secret; it made his conversion appear the more miraculous. What seems to have escaped notice is that he was no less obsessed with sex after conversion than he was before.

The rupture in Augustine's life between belief and practice and the unfortunate mending of that rip by a consistent ethic of distrust and avoidance have been responsible for cutting off generations of Christians from any healthy sense of ourselves as physical beings. We have learned from him to be obsessed with sex and to "live in two minds," dividing our "oughts" from our experiences.

4

The Rape of Marriage

It is 1968. Joyce and Matt have been married six years. They have four children; the oldest is five. Matt works two jobs to support the family; he keeps going because of what the priests and his mother have always taught him: if he works hard enough and long enough and keeps praying, God will provide for the growing number of mouths he has to feed. Any attempt to take charge of his family situation by employing some means of birth control fills him with self-contempt and guilt. The messages click on: "Trust God. God will send you the number of children you are supposed to have. How can you doubt God?" He does doubt when he struggles with bills or when he sees what Joyce is going through, but the old mantras and his growing workaholism combine to numb the uncertainty.

Joyce is depressed. She feels totally drained by the hours of work that four preschool children demand. She feels hopeless and alone: the partner she married is never at home, and she sees a growing gap in their positions. His many hours of overtime to earn money to pay the bills have earned him certain "perks" — new levels of professional competence and praise from peers in his field. She is too tired even to open a book and is becoming convinced that all she is "good for" is cleaning toilets and changing diapers. She wonders if the pope ever stayed up all night with sick children. But the pope said if she wants to be close to Matt she must permit another baby, and so she does. Moments of intimacy are clouded by fear and resentment. It doesn't make sense, and it's wearing her out, but the pope said she must, and so she does.

Twenty years ago it wasn't called "codependence." The pope made a formal statement reiterating that any Catholic married couple who used "artificial" forms of birth control (anything other than planned periods of abstinence) was guilty of mortal sin and deserving of hell. Couples who had been waiting for the statement and hoping for a different kind of answer were in anguish that they must continue to choose between pregnancy and separate rooms. The Vatican-approved "rhythm" method was about as dependable as holding one's breath and hoping: many who used "rhythm" found their ovulation cycles too irregular to predict any truly "safe" time for intercourse. But, nevertheless, there were couples who continued to use "Vatican roulette," because the pope said the choice was that or nothing.

Twenty-years ago it wasn't called "codependence," but couples who were already using pharmaceutical means of spacing pregnancies were hoping that a change in church law would bring an end to their oppressive feelings of guilt. Whatever the church said was received without question as the word of God. When the pope simply restated the old doctrine, they decided that they had no choice but to continue to "violate *God's* law" and live with the guilt rather than risk the added stress that another pregnancy would bring to the whole family.

Twenty years ago, we didn't call it "codependence," but both these groups thought their own perceptions of the meaning of marital love-making counted for nothing; the unmarried clerics who formed the decision-making body of the church had the sole right to say when and why and if their love-making was ethical, had any value, was anything more than sinful lust.

Twenty years ago, no one in the church was calling it "recovery," but many couples who heard that Vatican pronouncement finally said "no more." They began to talk with each other, allowed themselves the right to trust their own individual and collective experiences, gave themselves permission to make their own decisions and live by them. Those couples took a giant step out of codependence and into personal responsibility, though for some a twinge of guilt remained.

What had happened to cause so many couples to be so deeply codependent on church? Catholic marriages had been raped by the institutional church. In a church that claimed to loathe pleasure and prize pain, marriage was shamed, inherently flawed, hopelessly inadequate. To keep the devil in its place, the institution moved to pin marriage down and then proceeded to tighten the stranglehold. Marriage learned to see itself through the eyes of its captor and interiorized the contempt. It learned to distrust any of its own feelings, to depend on someone else to grant it any value at all. Marriage was overpowered, rendered helpless, shamed, cut off from its own experiences, and violated.

Those of us over thirty-five can remember early messages about sex and about ourselves that scarred self-worth, undermined our ability to trust our perceptions, and crippled our ability to form close relationships with others. The messages were sung with the old chorus of sin and shame and played in the background of every sexual thought and action, casting doubt and guilt on even the healthy steps of sexual development. The negative brainwashing — about the evils of sex — plays on through life, like a painful memory that always gets in the way.

The institutional church has raped marriages over and over: by encouraging members to remain in abusive marriages; by disdain for sexuality in general as evidenced by the neutering of the human form in church art and official garb; by its doctrine of virginity as the best or the only path to holiness, thereby robbing marriage of its own dignity and holiness; by giving Augustine and the unmarried clergy the right to write the rules for married life; and by controlling or suppressing the physical expression of committed love through sexual intimacy. Many of these may be particularly Catholic hang-ups; but the first — stand by your man, even in the face of abuse — is a strong tenet of some Protestant churches.

Churches who depend on the literal meaning of the English transla-tion of the Bible for answers to contemporary problems have encouraged married people to suffer through verbal or even physical abuse because it is "God's will." How many women have been advised to "stand by your man" and pray for him, so that he will "see the light of Christ" in them and not beat them anymore? How many are told to pray that God will change the heart of their spouse so that he will accept Christ as his savior and stop abusing the children?

Genderless Holiness

The statues of saints, in those churches that permit them, are reinforcing messages of bodiless dualism. The bodies of Jesus and the saints are uniformly straight, covered by identical gowns that fall straight from the shoulder in even folds. The faces are even the same — emotionless and asexual.

The statues do *not* say that true holiness is blind to gender, that both women and men are called to holiness. Men and women are *not* equal in these churches.

The underlying message is that all true virtue is neuter gender: men who have become neuter, women who have become neuter, and Jesus who also looks neuter.

The rest of the message is that you, the observer, are not like that, and therefore you are just ordinary, not holy. To be holy, you must give your center to the genderless, and try to follow their lead.

Some few churches or groups within churches still insist that those who hold office be genderless in their garb. What does it say about personal wholeness, about the incarnation of God in ordinary persons, if church officials are the only males in the culture who wear dresses and if the women in positions of respect must be draped from head to foot with what could be the slipcover of a chair? The current pope, John Paul II, has made it a personal crusade to convince women religious to return to the medieval gowns and veils. Today's children make sport of it all: "Never trust a man in a dress." They see it as an absurd anachronism. But we who grew up forty or more years ago, we who grew up accepting celibacy and neuter dress as a statement about *our* lives, got in line to give up our sexuality to be holy.

Virginity Means Virtue

When one of my children was preparing for confirmation, her teachers told her to choose a saint's name to add to her own. It was to be a person she admired and whose Christian example she wanted to emulate, as long as it was also a person long dead and duly canonized. When no one fitting all those specifications came to mind, I told her that, since she had already received a biblical name in baptism, no additional name was really necessary. It puts one in a difficult position, though, to take a stance different from the official policy — even adults have trouble with this — so I started looking for saints to suggest.

The first place I looked was an old missal containing a calendar of prayers for the feasts of the saints, along with little stories of each one. I was reminded of something I hadn't thought about in years: that the common denominators of "official" sainthood are virginity, clerical rank, or martyrdom.

Dick Westley put together an excellent developmental history of spirituality (see his *Theology of Presence*) in which he pointed out that for most of the history of Christianity, the only ones writing on spirituality were living a life of vowed celibacy. Few beyond the clerical elite had any education. And if someone else did show spiritual insight, the church "drafted" that person into the monastic ranks. Many Christian writers took the stance that sex was the enemy of spirituality.

Only recently do we have Christian people in committed intimate relationships, who are both theologically literate and openly appreciative of the spiritual depth of their own calling, who can speak and write and awaken a new dimension of appreciation of the depth of sexuality.

A few saints might have been married, but — thanks to "God's providence"! — they were widowed early so they could pursue the *true* path to sanctity by founding new religious orders.

Men hold the vast majority of saintly titles, most having lived as priests or as brothers in religious communities, and all of those presumably celibate. The exceptions among male saints are the early disciples of Jesus, who probably were married and did not consider themselves priests. But Catholic culture had dubbed them "the first priests," and, by reading their own body-spirit dualism back into first-century Jewish culture, assumed that they must have become celibate to follow Christ.

Monica, Augustine's mother, is evidence that codependence is officially recognized as a way of life meriting sainthood for women. And some have suggested that the ideal saintly woman is a dead virgin.

During the search-for-a-saint period, I visited a parish in our area that had just completed and opened its new church building. I was sitting toward the back and, before the service began, was observing the semicircular wall of stained glass windows that formed the back of the church. I noticed that the persons depicted in these windows were all males and all (Catholic-therefore-celibate) clergy. (To be accurate, there was one tiny woman religious, far in the background of a picture of a cleric giving communion to a child.) They were arranged in historical order from left to right, from the early missionaries to America to the present time.

I was dismayed to see that women and married people were not recognized as role models even in modern church art and architecture. Then I saw the last window.

The last image in the priestly sequence was the man who was the current pastor of the church — he had ordered his own unmistakable likeness rendered in stained glass — and, at *his* right hand, was the picture of the risen Christ. It was both appalling and ludicrous.

"I stand in the line of saints, and you do not." Catholics who are forty years old or more grew up with that constant message: celibacy equals virtue. Marriage is for those who cannot make the grade. Marriage is tainted, befouled with the pleasures of this world, but God will forgive you if you give us your center and judge your marriage according to our standards.

We were taught that marriage is permissible, good in the abstract, but that the "sexual part" — how did this get so fragmented! — is suspect, to be used sparingly and only for procreation. (Couples joke that a little more healthy passion in their marriages would be a blessing!)

We have been taught to distrust our own emotions — they are infected with concupiscence and lead us into sin — and so are dependent on the church to tell us the direction to God and glory. Cutting off one's own perceptions and living "in two minds" can lead to disastrous results.

Early Simplicity

Rigidity is a mark of an addictive system. The rigid marriage laws of the Roman Catholic church are indicators of the hierarchical addiction to power and the codependence of the members. Catholics have been taught not to trust their own experience, but to depend on the judgments of church officials instead. The marriage laws have held hurting people hostage for many generations.

Interestingly, the laws themselves evolved rather late in our history (1500s) and came about through a combination of political clout and negative attitudes toward sex that would never be accepted by today's Christians. A theology of marriage that was first the work of an abstinent but nonrecovering sex addict, that was later revised and rearticulated by celibate monks in monasteries, and was finally enacted into law to solve a civil problem and to assert the waning authority of the Roman hierarchy, has been presented by church authorities as coming straight from God.

The majority of church members, who were told nothing of the history, take the church's word that the laws are from God and struggle to live under them. For them, the only thing that makes marriage acceptable, perhaps "holy" in a diluted sort of way, is obedience to the clerically mandated laws.

Our lack of understanding of the origins of the marriage laws causes us to be less than confident in trusting the validity of our own experiences, causes us to measure ourselves against the standard of monks and find ourselves still-human-and-therefore-lacking. It causes us to cut out our center of judgment and hand it over to "holy mother church" and to function as automatons, robots, codependents. Understanding the evolution of the marriage laws can be a first step out of this type of codependence.

In the early church, there were no laws about marriage. The first generation of Christians was making a conscious move away from religious law and toward living the spirit, mission, and ministry of Jesus.

Instead of seeing Christianity as a new institution with new rubrics, they saw that following Jesus was a new dimension to life: a new depth, reaching out further, new motivations for action. Marriage, too, was seen as a way to live out this union with Jesus and with each other. And so it was encouraged that Christians choose their spouses from among the believers so they may better encourage one another in living their baptism. But this was a matter of suggestion rather than law.

There was no Christian marriage ceremony for the first few hundred years. Early generations of Christians exchanged vows according to the local secular customs: Greeks and Jews each followed their family traditions. Roman Christians followed Roman customs — the red veil, the man carrying the woman over the threshold — relics of old religious rites whose meanings were scarcely remembered even then.

The earliest record we have of a specifically Christian wedding rite dates from the fourth century, Augustine's era. It was from the community in Rome, was not mandatory, and was written for the wedding of a member of the clergy.

Fourth-century clergy were generally married. Because they were elected from within the local community, they were persons well known by all and recognized for living the message, persons whose marriage the whole community would want to celebrate — hence, the rite. But the fourth century was also a period when dualism was widely held and produced the first letters suggesting that married clergy abstain from sexual activity before leading the Eucharist. The transition in Christian thought was beginning.

The fifth century marked the end of the Roman empire, the end of civilization in Europe for a time, and with it a pause in academic and theological investigations. When those pursuits were dusted off again hundreds of years later, when theologians in monasteries began to ponder what makes a marriage a marriage, or what makes it a Christian marriage they consulted the books that were left from "the good old days," the many volumes of our good friend Augustine.

The medieval monks accepted the message from Ephesians that marriage symbolized a religious reality, but, like Augustine, tended to distrust the sexual element of married life. It was not until the twelfth century that theologians concurred that marriage was a sacrament, that the consent of two people in marriage created a symbol of the union of Christ with the church and was therefore an opportunity to "obtain" divine grace. Consent was still the only requirement for marriage; the church did not impose a rite.

And Finally, the Laws

Laws mandating church involvement in or supervision of marriage are only four centuries old — four out of twenty. For the first sixteen centuries of Western Christianity, though it was encouraged that Christians marry "in the fold" and though it became no longer rare to exchange vows at the church, it was recognized as every person's right to marry whom they chose and to do so by common consent alone.

In the sixteenth century, as the Reformation and the first stirrings of nationalism began to break up Rome's religious and political empire, Rome convened the Council of Trent, a Counter-Reformation council whose purpose was to stem the tide out of the Roman church by correcting some of the most blatant abuses and by reasserting authority in religious matters. At this point, Rome took to itself the right to legislate marriage.

The reformers — Luther et al. — stood for the authority of Scripture, the sufficiency of personal faith in God, and, originally, for the priesthood of all believers. The council of Catholic bishops at Trent was making the opposite points: the absolute authority of the Roman hierarchical structure, the need for *their* church rituals to connect one with God, and the indispensable role of the ordained clergy.

The council was not in the frame of mind to work out a theology of marriage, and no one in the Roman camp was disputing what was in the books anyway: what the twelfth-century monks had done with the fourth-century writings of Augustine was just fine with the bishops. The question on the docket was this: what shall we do (we who hold all civil and religious authority!) to deal with the problem of marriage vows pledged in secret? If one of the partners deserted or if a dispute arose later, the civil-ecclesiastical authorities did not have enough evidence to decide the case.

The bishops discussing the problem seemed to concur that the solution lay in requiring some proof. The consensus was to demand witnesses — but how many? Many of the bishops voted for two witnesses as sufficient to attest that a marriage had taken place.

The issue was settled by enacting a policy that both addressed the problem of secret marriages and made a point of the council's pet causes: the necessity of structure, ritual, and ordained priesthood. The council insisted that, for the Roman church to consider a marriage valid, the following would be required: exchange of vows before three witnesses, one of whom must be an ordained Roman Catholic priest.

I can almost see them brushing the dust off their hands when they were done with the whole nasty subject. Now on to dividing the empires of Europe and the gold of the New World!

Annulments as Abuse

The annulment process, in its current juridical mode, is an ongoing violation of marriage.

An annulment is a document stating that there never was a marriage: some factor, present from the very beginning, precluded the possibility of a valid commitment.

Annulment is based on these assumptions, most written into law at Trent: a marriage (between any two baptized Christians, not just Catholics) is considered valid if the couple exchanged vows before a Roman cleric and two other witnesses and if both parties possessed the psychological ability at that time to give consent; every "valid" marriage is considered a sacrament, a sign of the union between Jesus and humankind, an event that speaks to the world of the saving love of God; every "valid" marriage must, therefore, be permanent.

Given these assumptions, to allow a second marriage, church officials, they say, must prove the first union never was a marriage. When a couple appears with a broken marriage, the church can only put it in one of two categories: either there were factors there in the beginning that marred the consent and marked it for downfall, in which case the vows could not have been valid and it never was a marriage; or it was a valid marriage, and therefore it still is a valid marriage, and if they attempt to marry someone else, they will be guilty of sin.

There are some pieces missing in the "logic" of church marriage laws: people who were baptized as infants do not necessarily consider the Christian faith central to their adult lives and may not consider their marriage to be a commitment to a role of sacramental responsibility. Marriage is relational, never static, so it cannot point to God in spite of itself, and it certainly cannot be a sign of sacred union when the relationship itself has become destructive.

The annulment process consists of the submission of an extensive questionnaire on the history of the relationship, including written affidavits from others who knew the couple and a personal interview by a member of the church court, the tribunal. It takes the tribunal about two years to process the case and costs around $850. The fee varies from diocese to diocese, and can be waived, in whole or in part, in cases of need. That is the "good news."

The "bad news" is that even the standard fee is an assessment levied against hurting people "to help them get right with God," as if their relationship with God depends on their submission to the church court. The fee goes to help pay the cost of maintaining the court that judges them, funds that could better be used for counseling.

In some dioceses, there are political games: it is no secret that those who "know someone" get more expeditious handling. Some have been told that a larger "donation" would hasten the process; others have found their annulment "delayed" until payment was complete.

The Roman church insists that Catholics may not remarry after a failed marriage or, if they have already remarried, may not participate in the sacraments unless they have sought and obtained an official church annulment of the first marriage.

One woman was upset that she was could not participate when her young daughter received communion for the first time. Her church, Roman Catholic, insisted that it should annul her husband's first marriage before she could take part. But he was Episcopalian and thought it overbearing that they should require that. She was caught in the middle, with her church exerting pressure on her marriage rather than supporting it.

It used to be that annulments were rarely granted. But today, even though the definition of annulment remains the same, they are rarely denied. Even in cases where it is clear that there was a valid commitment, and the relationship was a good marriage for years before addiction or adultery brought it down, the marriage is still declared null — it never happened. The institution is not really making a determination about the marriage as much as putting people through an act of submission to Holy Mother.

As more types of cases are being granted annulments, the hierarchy continues to sidestep the larger question of whether they ought to be sitting in judgment of marriages at all.

Can We Annul the Institutional Church?

Picture this. People who have vowed to live in faithful covenant with each other are ushered into the room. They have failed in that covenant and are here to give an accounting of that failure in the hopes that the powers-that-be will wipe this sad scene from the records and give them another chance.

They begin their sad tale. For years there has been no trust, no respect, no mutuality in this relationship. One partner has become increasingly autocratic, domineering, even abusive; the other has gradually lost her identity, her ability to function, her will to live. Control has replaced cooperation, manipulation has conquered respect.

There is even evidence that one partner exhibits the behaviors common to the established phase of addiction and refuses to seek recovery; he has abandoned the family to struggle with their issues alone, returning sporadically to harass or abuse. The other partner's behavior is codependent, jeopardizing her mental and physical health. While they are not destitute, one partner squanders the family funds on his addiction, while the other has to scrimp and scrape to nourish the children. The children are confused and acting out the family stress in a number of hurtful ways.

The judges listen to the testimony, pore over the written affidavits, discuss the matter among themselves. Clearly, this family is dysfunctional, everyone is being harmed, and there is no hope of reconciliation since one partner remains recalcitrant. There are certainly sufficient grounds for annulment.

We have just annulled the church.

Church is probably our largest covenant community, our largest extended family, and it has become dysfunctional in all the ways a family can be dysfunctional. Some parties are addicted to power; others are codependent to the point of self-destruction. One side insists on respect, but does not offer it in return; it demands adherence to a strict set of rules for covenant fidelity, but feels free to live by another.

A marriage is the smallest covenant community; it stands within the larger covenant communities of church and families of origin. The couple learns to relate to each other from those church and parental families. They learn dysfunctional behaviors from the church and parental families, too.

Both marriage and church are called to be sacrament, a sign that speaks Jesus' love to the world, as should our sharing of the Lord's Supper. But how can a regal church represent a humble man walking barefoot with the poor, washing others' feet, and insisting there be "no lording it over one another"?

Perhaps now we can see the absurdity of the annulment process. If a marriage fails, should we put that marriage in the pillory, gather the powers-that-be, and make careful examination of all the details of their failure? After all, the powers-that-be, the judges, are themselves one of the key families that taught them domination and codependence. Shall we grant the "powers" the right to pass judgment on the couple, to say there never was a covenant, never was a sacrament, when the "powers" have long been failing in the very same ways? Shall we make married couples scapegoats for the whole community's failure to live out a covenant of mutual respect and support?

The history of the decisions that created the annulment process should be enough to invalidate the process. The reasons for establishing it would never be accepted as healthy reasons today. But most people do not know the reasons why things are the way they are.

Do couples who seek an annulment do so because the church says that without that certificate they are cut off from God, or do they really need some help closing the door on a failed marriage? Is the need imposed from outside or generated from within?

That we accept without question the need for this elaborate process to "get right with God," is itself a sign of our codependence; it is so hard to separate God from the institution. If it weren't for the codependence of our church system, the annulment process would have been abandoned or boycotted long ago, replaced with something more effective and less demeaning.

This system would not continue without codependence. Only a co-dependent membership would grant this tribunal the right to add their judgment to what the applicants already know — especially in cases where former spouses have already remarried and moved on — that the marriage is dead. In large, loosely connected parishes, it is unlikely that the pastor would even know that someone is in a second marriage unless that person chose to reveal it or decided to ask permission.

Granted, the process of looking at the causes of marital breakdown can be very helpful if done with skilled help, and some individuals who received no counseling at the tribunal still found that they grew just by telling their story. But there are other more helpful contexts for doing that.

Beyond the Need for a Juridical Process

If the need that brings people to seek an annulment is generated from within, if those applying truly want additional help processing the end of the relationship or finding reassurance that God will no longer hold them responsible for living up to this covenant, there are other means to achieve that end. Other means already exist for achieving both these goals: group counseling, one-on-one counseling, work with a spiritual director, support groups for the divorced, marriage encounter groups for support in second marriages.

Other church-related processes can be developed: opportunities for looking at one's family of origin and other emotional "baggage" brought into the first marriage, so that there is no more "fighting monsters in the dark"; rites of reconciliation in which community members actively assist each other to experience God's and the community's forgiveness and acceptance, as in the fifth step of the Twelve Step program (see chapter 12); a rite that might be used by a divorced individual in the presence of a caring, supportive community, to mark prayerfully the closure of an important period of one's life and the passage to a new period of growth. Neither goal — processing the divorce nor one's relationship with God — depends on a church judgment that there never was a marriage, a judgment that theoretically can go either way but in fact always goes the same way, a judgment that often belies the person's own experience and gets in the way of facing the truth and finding healing.

There are many who are in second marriages without annulments, who have thought through the issues, done the processing, gotten support, and have decided that a church annulment would add nothing to their relationship with their spouse or with God. They have stepped out of their child's role in church and given themselves permission *not* to seek an annulment. They have given themselves permission to continue participating in their community without it.

As people come to grips with their own codependence on church, they are less willing to subject themselves to that process. Couples and individuals look more often now to private or group assistance to correct the patterns that led to the breakup of their first marriages, and they seek community support to live responsibly in a second marriage, without also buying into an institutional piece of paper that will always say what the subscribers want it to say: this marriage is dead. Some clerics even encourage people to seek counseling and have taken a stand against church policy by refusing to initiate or process any more annulments.

Wouldn't it make more sense to sit down together as struggling people — not the value-givers and the value-less — in a home rather than the diocesan tribunal, and try to sort out the mistakes we have made, the amends we need to make, the lessons we can learn, and the steps we can take toward healthy relationships — whether we have experienced a failed marriage or a righteous-looking but equally failed church?

Birth Control — a Codependent Issue

The upheaval that occurred with the 1968 publication of *Humanae Vitae*, the papal letter on birth control, was the turning point for many of us in our understanding of church as a network of divine authority and a step for some out of codependence.

At the end of the Second Vatican Council, a team of physicians, psychologists, and theologians was commissioned to make a thorough investigation of the issue of family planning, and particularly the use of pharmaceutical means to control conception, long a Roman taboo. After a lengthy consideration from every side of the issue, the commission submitted its report, recommending that the church (still the voice of divine authority) amend its directives to the faithful to include permission — under certain circumstances and within the family — to use pharmaceutical means to control conception.

The pope, Paul VI, read the report and issued *Humanae Vitae:* the commission cites noble reasons why a couple might desire to limit the size of their family; however, our venerable father Augustine said, and the church has always taught, that any means of controlling conception save abstinence are mortally sinful (deserving eternal punishment in hell). Therefore, we have no choice but to reiterate that position.

Catholics instinctively know there is something wrong here, but few have the information or the confidence to "hold their own" while contesting a papal mandate. I hope this book will provide both.

The primitive notion of conception was that the male seed was already a miniature human, needing only a fertile place to grow. Not until the invention of the microscope in the seventeenth century was it understood that conception was the union of *two* cells and that women contributed more than a "fertile field."

Tracking ovulation cycles to have intercourse at "safe" times — the "rhythm method" that the Catholic church now advocates — was unknown in ancient times. Clearly it would *not* have been acceptable to Augustine; his position on birth control was absolute: intercourse, even in marriage, was only for making babies. Any other intent, or any pleasure, rendered it sinful.

And finally, we Christians are heir to some very unhealthy attitudes toward sex. To continue to make those misunderstandings the norm for Christian sexual ethics, without any consideration for historical context or the more recent development of psychology, makes as much sense as using fourth-century norms for current medical practice.

The experience of the Catholic married community in the wake of *Humanae Vitae* was like Dorothy discovering that Oz was just a man — a very good man, perhaps, but a very poor wizard.

There were changes during the 1960s that all pointed beyond the absolute Roman authority to something more basic — Scripture, the experience of the earliest communities of Christians, the wisdom of *all* the people of God, and, in the context of all these, the individual conscience. To people who had grown in the security of memorized answers to all ethical questions, asking permission in any case of doubt, this was a whole new set of rules and responsibilities. The birth control question forced the issue, and many married couples chose responsibility over security, responsible independence over codependence.

There are some Catholic couples who choose to use contraceptives, but see themselves as disobedient, breakers of the law: maybe God will punish us, but we have to do it this way. They still remain cut off from their own experiences and feelings and define themselves by a standard outside themselves.

But for others, church could no longer mean passive membership, blind obedience, "pray, pay, and obey." There was wisdom in the people, and healing, too. In a very real sense, we were discovering through experience that we *are* church and beginning to recover from at least one kind of codependence.

Overall, however, there is an institutional obsession with sexual matters. Popes and bishops have been peering into bedrooms, examining marriages under microscopes, and assigning faithful couples who felt ill prepared to be good parents to nurture an unlimited number of children. They have remained blind to the larger issues of church-endorsed injustice, misogynism, and the modeling of family dysfunction on the institutional level.

What does this say to married Catholics? If they follow the directives of their pope, they must maintain the split between their own experience and the teaching of their hierarchy: between their own feelings and thoughts and their actions. They must accept the verdict that their experiences are not legitimate, numb their awareness with the mantra of "God's will," and act on the pope's judgment, even when it violates their own. That is codependence.

5

Double Lives

His name is Phil. He is a priest. He entered the seminary at thirteen, just out of eighth grade, and he has been in the system ever since. He did not have much to do with girls during high school. He knew he would have to live without them to be a priest, so he figured he would be better off not getting involved with them. When it would have been age-appropriate to be growing in an awareness of his sexuality and his ability to relate to women, Phil was encouraged to avoid any thought of or contact with the "dangerous" gender. Besides, his time and attention were full of other things.

He idolized the young charismatic priests who were his instructors; he spent as much time with them as possible and imagined himself someday receiving that kind of admiration. His after-school hours were scheduled for him too — sports with the other seminarians, service projects in the neighborhoods, field trips with the priests. His involvement made him feel part of a special group that was somehow above the rest, a group on whom the world depended to be brought closer to God.

When he was ordained, he embarked enthusiastically on his mission to spread the good news of the gospel and to help the hurting. His first assignment was carefully chosen by the seminary board to be a good experience: the pastor was very personable, the parishioners were economically comfortable, with time and energy to invest in social events that raised large sums to give to the poor. He felt like a hero; everything he touched turned to gold. And everyone seemed to love one another.

Also on staff was a young woman religious named Margaret. She was in charge of religious education and called on Father Phil's assistance to present ideas to the parents or give a warm, approachable image of the church to the children. He was pleased to have a co-worker with the same vision of church; it made it that much easier to achieve his dream.

At thirty-four, he was moved to his second parish. The pastor there was totally disenchanted with the whole business. He "did his priestly duty" on Sundays, spent most of his time alone in his room, and drank to forget how dead he felt. Anything Phil did or suggested disturbed the hum-drum, business-as-usual routine and generally meant more work, and so Phil's projects were routinely vetoed. Dinnertime in the rectory was dominated by the television set, and Phil's leading questions to engage the pastor in conversation were met with pompous pronouncements — very final in tone — or with uninterested grunts.

Phil was stuck. He couldn't throw himself into his work because the pastor blocked him at every turn. He stewed in his room, trying to figure out ways to get around a dead pastor. He tried a new approach with some young couples in the parish, only to be called on the carpet by his boss. He tried again.

He began, at thirty-five, to work his way through his own adolescence, the emotional work that other teenagers were doing while he was in seminary. While other teens were testing their boundaries with parents, his parents had already started to treat him with deference. He identified with the law-givers, with the decision-makers, in a system where they defined the only right.

Phil was confused. He had been so right, so sure, for so long. Life was mapped out for him; everything was clear. The authority problems of other adolescents had looked so juvenile to him; after all, he *was* part of the authority structure. Now — why now! — everything was becoming muddled. The closed world of the seminary that made "God's will" so clear and so easy was nothing like the real world in which he had to minister. The "loving fraternity of all other priests" was a joke. The pastor certainly didn't share his dream, didn't even respect him. Now he had to learn how to handle the boundary issues that would define who he was and what set him apart from others; he even had to define what distinguished him from other priests.

Phil was alone. He started visiting his old parish on days off. Margaret was happy to have Phil visit her classes, and there was time afterward for a cup of coffee and real conversation with someone who still did believe in the dream. Those Wednesday visits became the high point of Phil's week.

Phil invited Margaret to coordinate a segment of his parish's education program, to try to breathe some life into it. The pastor didn't like it, but Phil had learned how to time his requests carefully to avoid the pastor's wrath. Margaret was well received by the people, and the presence of two enthusiastic leaders gave some of them permission to respond. Phil's hope was rekindled.

Phil turned to Margaret for a listening ear, for comfort and consolation, for someone to share his dream, for someone with whom he could make things happen. And, sooner or later, things began to happen to Phil and Margaret.

For the first time in his almost four decades, Phil had to face some bewildering experiences. He had never fallen in love before; he had never been interested in girls. The preadolescent, just-us-guys attitude had carried him all the way through his teens and twenties and into his thirties. Now he couldn't get Margaret out of his mind and couldn't imagine Margaret out of his life. They worked together, planned together, dreamed together, were saving the world together — and they were sleeping together.

Phil was in the middle of a terrible dilemma. He had always wanted to be a priest. He had signed on at thirteen and bought the whole program. He never had to face the struggles of adolescence until he was on the other side of thirty, never felt the need to question anything till he was going on middle age. He had, without hesitation, promised obedience and celibacy as absolute conditions for his priesthood, yet now he felt the need to break them both to be a better priest. He spent more and more time at Margaret's apartment. When he was not with her, he was in his private agony of loneliness and hypocrisy.

The bishop of his diocese seemed sensitive to these issues and invited all the priests of Phil's class to a retreat to discuss them. Phil bravely presented his problem, but no one ventured a response. "Does anyone else have something to share?" asked the facilitator, ignoring Phil's plea and scanning the faces. No one spoke. In the talk that followed, the bishop said that he appreciated the fact that his men had certain needs, and he didn't care if they took care of those needs, just as long as they were discreet and kept things quiet. And keeping things quiet, Phil concluded, meant no public confessions to fellow priests, either.

Eunuchs for the Kingdom

The dilemma many clerics face is the choice between a life that is open, honest, and "sexually integrated" (an ambiguous and sometimes misleading label), and their own codependence on church, the choice between claiming their own opinions and decisions, and holding tight to the hand of "Holy Mother."

Codependence means that we depend on someone else to say we are good, valuable, one of the special few, and that we will sacrifice our own ideas, opinions, right to make decisions, and any form of autonomy to maintain that position. In a church that puts clerics on a pedestal and defines them as eunuchs for the kingdom, clerics who want to stay on the pedestal had better look like eunuchs.

John Bradshaw talks about an inner split as a cause of codependence. He says we divide into two selves, the public self and the private self. The self we show to others is the self our system will accept — ruled by intellect, buying the system's values. The other part, the self that feels, that has an emotional life that the system condemns as evil, becomes the inner self, hidden from public view, buried.

It is the clergy of some churches who are under greatest pressure to live as if the body and spirit were split. They are almost *required* to give up their centers and become stereotypes — is this not the purpose of "formation"? In some churches, the leaders feel they must present a public self who is a saint, and a saint is defined as one having no sexual problems or, better yet, no sexual life.

A church that is a codependent system will pressure the cleric from inside and out, top and bottom, to maintain that perfect, asexual public image. He feels pressure from within himself: he has given his center over to his overseer or bishop and to his congregation; he derives his sense of value from their approval and might lose it all if he let his real self be known.

The bishop, too, has given his center over to the system, and that system would be devalued by a scandal involving lower-level clergy, so he will want to see only their perfect public selves.

And finally, the congregation has given some or all of their centers over to this local cleric and to the church structure for which he stands. They have delegated this cleric to be their "holy person," for it is easier to own one than to be one, and they cannot let him step down off his pedestal.

In a community where no one has a secure center, everyone has a vested interest in maintaining the façade. In a community that has shut off its feelings, the leaders cannot admit even to having any. They are therefore at greatest risk of becoming codependent.

The most obvious application of Augustinian dualism is Catholicism's mandatory celibacy. The most hidden cases are those of pedophiles and sex addicts of all denominations whose churches are in denial, whose churches are covering up and enabling that behavior rather than facing it and encouraging treatment.

Celibacy is not a problem to everyone. The single life can certainly be healthy if it is balanced. Not every cleric whose job requires a pledge of celibacy would marry (or choose a committed homosexual relationship) if given the opportunity. There are a variety of reasons for this.

A few have found a healthy balance — a sense of self-worth and independence, personal satisfaction in work, a close community for support, healthy outlets for fun — and are content with their lives as they are. For these individuals, intimacy is well developed, though not focused on any one other person and not expressed genitally. Their parental drive is achieved though the creative energies they invest in their work, both with people and with ideas. Celibacy can be a healthy lifestyle. The point I am making is that it is not chosen by many in our society, it is not the true choice of most in church service, and the healthy fruition of celibacy does not come through mandating it.

Some, who have not found that healthy balance, are still not bothered by the celibacy requirement because they are "married" to the power they feel they have as one of an elite core — the dispensers of the treasures of God. This is the role they signed on for, their major persona, the source of their self-worth. For some, it occupies the center of their lives and conceals any need for intimacy.

Some have become Lone Rangers; the seminary system trained them in this role. They have "walled off" their inner selves so well that they do not "hear" their own deeper feelings and are not capable of sharing with anyone on an intimate level.

Some are not content with celibacy at all, but have learned to medicate their discontent so that it no longer bothers them. These individuals numb their pain with alcohol, workaholism, or some other compulsive behavior so that they do not have to confront the question of intimate relationships, or make choices about it.

So celibacy is not a problem to all who are required to take that pledge.

What happens with those who are not at peace and whose inner selves are aware of that discontent, rather than "walled off" or numbed? If the public self must remain celibate and untainted by any suggestion of sexuality, what does one do with an inner self that does not want to be untouched and untouchable? One faces a very difficult choice.

In the choice between the assassination of the public self — the ascetic stereotype that is the source of one's self-worth — and annihilation of the smaller but tenacious private self, either choice is self-destructive. Either option feels like suicide. Codependence is what backs us into these corners, what robs us of choice. If we knew that we were whole persons in and of ourselves and understood that God loves us as the persons we are on the inside, then we could choose to use our talents in the institutional setting or not. But if our whole worth depends on someone or something outside ourselves, if we are codependents within this system, we are quite helpless.

Behind Closed Doors

Some of the clergy, who feel they are caught between two impossible choices, try to solve the dilemma by making a third but equally self-destructive choice. They give up the attempts to integrate the two selves: they live a double life. They choose to maintain the public façade of the committed ascetic, often decrying the sexual misdeeds of others, while at the same time living a secret life with a lover or engaging in casual couplings with random partners.

For obvious reasons, there are no statistics on this. But people who work closely with and within the system estimate the proportion of truly celibate men in the Roman Catholic clergy to range from 50 percent down to 10 percent.

One well-respected cleric, speaking at a priests' retreat, said that mandatory celibacy leaves them few choices. The easiest is to become workaholic or alcoholic (to "numb out"), and the number of burnt-out or alcoholic priests points to this as the favorite option of many. The ideal choice, but most difficult to accomplish, is the establishment of an open, deeply personal, mutually supportive relationship with a small community. And the third choice is made by more clerics than any of us would guess — to have a lover.

In an institution that insists on celibacy, there is a lot going on behind closed doors. The unspoken policy for priests of at least one diocese is: "Get your needs met, but keep it quiet." "Quiet" is a relative term and covers all sorts of tactics. For the cautious, there are weekend junkets to big cities: see a play and pick up or hire a lover. No one knows your name or your title. The very bold have moved a mistress or gay lover into the rectory. She may also function as the housekeeper or religious education director; he may be a young seminarian or another priest. It is not too obvious; those who do not want to see, who do not want to know, can look the other way.

These shifts are rationalized a hundred different ways: "Let's face it," some say, "the church needs priests — right? They need *me*. I don't want to add to the priest-shortage, so I'll just keep this quiet." "I didn't know what intimacy was when I made those promises. And now that I do, I'm too old to make a career change. So I'll be discreet." The reasoning isn't bad, but it is codependent. Codependence says, "I must have this role in this closed system or I am no one; therefore, I have no other choice." And as long as the individuals are codependent, their choices will not be healthy.

Some acknowledge that celibacy is not the best way for them to grow as healthy and whole individuals but want to continue to minister, so they "redefine" their vows to mean chaste within one faithful relationship. Some Roman clerics consider celibacy to apply only to relationships with women; gay relationships "do not count," are not seen as a violation of their vow.

Some of these men in clandestine relationships are just trying to devise a facsimile of "normal life" using the available components of a sick system. They are victims, in a sense, and perceive themselves as trapped in the dysfunction. At the same time, by these choices, they are contributing to the isolation and secrecy that enables dysfunction to continue.

Isolation

One of the problems with any kind of double life is that one lives in isolation — the opposite of Christian community! If one is in an ongoing intimate relationship with one person, that requires support.

Even in marriage, which has the benefit of being public, there can be great harm caused by isolation. Couples *need* a community to witness to fidelity, to encourage them through the rough times, to celebrate the joy of being together. It is very difficult, even in marriage, to overcome the tendency to withdraw from community in times of trouble, to pull away from support at the very times we need it most.

Those in secret, double-life relationships are doubly isolated: deprived of community support and denied any comfort from each other when others are around. Since no one should know that they are intimates, their public selves must remain aloof, professionally distant from each other. The special little exchanges that keep love alive are taboo anywhere where others might see. When they have worked through some of their own obstacles to intimacy, there is no group with whom they can celebrate the joys of union.

Secret, double-life unions are frequently doubly codependent. They remain secret because the clerics have given their centers to "holy mother church," and they continue for years because the lovers have given their centers to the priests. Neither can risk facing life without the one who holds their center, and it would mean taking a big risk to move this clandestine, unsupported relationship into the light of day.

Imagine what would happen if either partner started to recover from codependence. Imagine the lover saying: "I love you very much. I treasure our time together and the ways we have each grown in our years together. But I want to be with you more than once in a while. I have spent much of the last five years waiting for you to call. I am always there when you need me, but I cannot depend on you to be there when I need you. Sometimes, when I would like to be with you, you are afraid to be seen with me. I need to have an equal commitment, and one I can build a future on. Will you love me in the open or not?"

This is healthy. Love is strong; responsibility is mutual. But a codependent could not say this, or would take it back within the hour.

Imagine the cleric saying to the parish or to the bishop: "I have served this church faithfully for the last ten years. You have affirmed me in the work I have done, and I am grateful to you for that. But I want you to understand that, during these last years, I have found someone whom I love very much and who loves me. I feel I can grow as a person and serve the community better if I can share my dreams and my struggles, my life, with one person intimately, as many of you are doing. I would like your support for our union, and for ours to be a support to your own, and so we plan to live here. I will go on serving this community with the talents God has given me, one way or another, and will continue in my work in this parish if you want me. It is up to you: will you continue in our relationship now that I will no longer be single?"

A pastor did make that announcement to his parish once. The parishioners cheered him, but the bishop removed him. (That brings up more questions about our codependence in church: how does it happen that a community will stand by while a bishop "removes" the pastor whom they have chosen?)

Unfortunately, most double-lifers cannot risk facing life without "holy mother church," cannot imagine being a whole adult person, a caring and effective minister, apart from the system. They continue in their codependence to church, their lovers in their codependence to them, while pressure and fear of discovery erode their relationship and their professional effectiveness. The same factors also erode their self-esteem: it is a shame-based relationship.

Using People

Another problem with sex-on-the-side is that it fosters the attitude that women or gay men are there to be used, to perform a sexual service with no reciprocal commitment of any kind from the "celibate" clergyperson. Among some members of the "brotherhood," there is a callous disregard for the other person involved. "If you need a woman, go away for a while and have some women. Get it out of your system, but don't leave the priesthood because of them." "We will take care of the woman for you; forget about her and get back to work."

In the Roman church, at least, there is a strong correlation between the attitude that women and gay men are there for priests to use as sex partners with no reciprocal commitment, and the attitude that women and gay men have less value as persons, few ideas worth listening to, and no rights in the church. As in Augustine's case, it is difficult to determine which came first: do they use women "to get their needs met" because they learn in church that women are just their servants, or do they treat women as servants in church because they have already bedded and left them and have ceased regarding them as persons?

The official policy bears certain similarities to the profile of perpetrators of sexual abuse: regarding others as sex objects, using others to get their needs met, covering up sexual activity, ensuring silence by intimidation. The continuation of this policy fosters and enables the tendency toward sexual abuse. Like everything else in addictive family systems, this scenario will continue until we say "enough!"

Codependents will sometimes suspend their own moral values to maintain the relationship on which they have hung their identity. Some clerics can preach on the connection between sexual activity and mutual personal responsibility, but have suspended or completely lost that connection in their own sexual encounters. In fact, some preach more strongly when they are trying to get their own sexual lives under control.

While the codependence of the clerics on the institution precludes their admitting their problem and getting help, the codependence of the lovers on the clerics also perpetuates the unhealthy situation. "But it is not Father Jim's fault that he has to sneak around this way. If only the church would let him marry me!" Some are repeatedly drawn toward the relationship precisely because it will *not* work, choosing a cleric for the same reasons they might choose to have an affair with a married man. The only way out of codependence is responsibility, not for the behavior or misbehavior of someone else, but for our own choices and actions. That applies to both the errant clerics and the women and men they bed.

There has been a lot written and said in recent years about how celibates can and should "integrate their sexuality." Some of the advice is healthy, advocating deep personal friendships with both sexes and developing both the masculinity and femininity that coexist in every one of us. What is overlooked, however, is the deep contradiction between the kind of intimacy they seek and the proscription on that closeness they have grudgingly accepted. Most of the audience have no personal inclination to be sexually abstinent. Most of those who made that commitment of celibacy would not have chosen to live that way were it not a requirement for public service in their church.

For most now struggling with a commitment of celibacy, true integration of sexuality would mean developing those deep personal friendships, allowing one of those friendships to blossom, becoming open enough (psychologically naked) and generous enough (mutually generative) that that relationship itself becomes a source of life, and eventually giving sexual expression to the love and unity they share with that one other person.

A pattern of dining out with a woman and masturbating alone later is not "integrating one's sexuality." Weekend lovers in distant cities, or one night stands at gay bars at home, are not ways to "integrate one's sexuality." They are examples of aborting one's sexual development short of maturity, short of mutuality, short of integration with the whole of one's life. And it is the codependence of the whole system that maintains the pattern.

While celibacy vs. pseudo-celibacy may be a Catholic problem, there are clergy of all denominations whose private selves are in trouble and more and more at odds with their public selves because of the system's inability to deal with intimacy. In pseudo-celibacy cases, the errant behavior might be considered acceptable by society but against church law; however in other cases, the behaviors in question are not accepted at all, and may even violate civil or criminal law. In the celibacy cases, individuals exhibit codependence — clerics to church, and the lovers to the clerics. But in these more troublesome cases, the whole system is codependent, operating like the prime enabler in an addictive family, covering up even criminal behavior to "save" the reputation of the family.

The helping professions have a taboo against sexual involvement with clients. The level of psychological intimacy reached in these situations can make sexual closeness very tempting, and yet sexual contact violates the professional relationship like incest violates a family relationship. In a closed church system that does not admit to the possibility of sexual problems, clergy who do get into adulterous, promiscuous, addictive relationships with parishioners or others cannot get help.

How many clerics, married or celibate, Protestant or Catholic, have become sexually involved with members of their congregations, particularly with individuals they have counseled or comforted? Because the denominational administrations, and church members as well, act as codependent enablers in the system, cases rarely come to light. There is almost never long-term help for the cleric involved, just a quick move to cover the evidence.

How many clerics have fallen in love with a stricken widow or an abused wife, seeing the possibility of being able to rescue and care for and love a family they have begun to help. But marriages built on the foundation of one partner's strength and need to rescue and the other's dependence and need to adore are headed for rocky ground. Churches need to address the inherent codependence of such relationships — where one relies on needy people to fill the hole in oneself — and deal with them in one-on-one counseling. But to confront one-up-one-down individual relationships, the churches would first have to come to terms with the same pattern in clergy-laity relations.

Pedophilia

What if a seminary system does not allow healthy development of one's sexuality and the church-family system refuses to deal with the sexual issues of its ordained? What if the church leadership does not foster clerical openness about sexuality on an adult level — coming to terms with one's orientation, nurturing one's needs for psychological intimacy, and satisfying the need for physical touch with one's peers. We seem to have a disproportionately large number of church staff who "need" to be sexual with dependent persons, particularly children.

Those who work with victims and survivors of childhood sexual abuse have to be very clear about two issues: when adults are sexual with children, either physically or emotionally sexual, it is always considered abuse, and it is always the adult's fault — always. Naming the abuse properly and putting the responsibility where it belongs are critically important in helping a child or an adult-child to heal.

My friend Linda Dunn pointed out to me that the term "pedophilia" misses the mark, avoiding responsibility and ignoring the enormous violation of trust perpetrated against children. Since clerics are in such a trusted position — the confidant of both parents and children, presented to the children as their spiritual parent, even called "Father" in some denominations — acts of sexual abuse of children by clergy should be named for the horrendous violations of trust that they are — "incest." And the incest is being denied, covered up, left untreated, and allowed to continue.

In one case, a cleric who seemed to be an exceptionally good youth pastor was found to be sexually involved with a young adolescent. The family threatened court action, but agreed to drop the charges against the church on the condition that he be moved. And moved he was — to another church where he has been given charge of another youth group!

In a rural diocese, a cleric was tried and convicted of pedophilia and sent to prison to serve time for it. The church took steps to erase him from history: he officially never happened! The small diocese paid a million dollars in damages to the family. A million dollars for incest is hard to disguise in the church budget; would it be listed as "rectory expenses"? Where did the money come from? Some slush fund? Other budgets? A bigger tin box from a bigger diocese? Someone knows, the one who ordered it done and others who covered it up, and those persons are continuing the lie. The imprisoned man himself receives a regular payment from his former diocese, payment for his silence, which he has been told will be discontinued if he ever makes his story public.

If a lay person committed the crime of this priest, would he not be subject to public outrage? Yet church institutions bury the evidence while the church members look the other way: codependent family systems are good at keeping secrets.

Double Lives — Sexual Addiction

Double lives are compounded by sexual addiction. The seminary system and clerical life in general seem to be fertile ground for the development of sexual addiction: candidates are caught between the pressure to be perfect and the proscription against any kind of intimacy with others, between overemphasis on sex — albeit negative attention — and the repression of all legitimate sexual expression.

In 1983, Patrick Carnes brought sexual addiction into the light with his book *Out of the Shadows*. In 1989, Carnes followed with *Contrary to Love: Helping the Sexual Addict*, in which he describes the development of sexual addiction. "In the earliest phase, sexual behavior that is a precursor to addiction is difficult, if not impossible, to distinguish from normal sexual behavior.... Many addicts, however, report that the impact of these early activities was exceptionally intense.... Also, addicts can often recall that self-stimulation was not merely experimentation; it was already a way to anesthetize emotional pain" (52, 53).

He goes on to describe certain environments that can foster the addiction: "Addicts who are professionals in various fields report that their addictions started and flourished during their training experiences — medical school, seminary, law school, graduate school. The demands of the curriculum, the competitive pressure to be one of the 'survivors,' and the high expectations of the family were coupled with lack of structure — a great deal of unscheduled time and only periodic accountability, when tests and papers were due" (54).

In the 1960s and before, years when large numbers applied and were told "many are called but few are chosen," the pressure in seminaries was intense. There was heavy emphasis on behavioral perfection and academic achievement and a need to prove oneself by achieving the goal of ordination. Candidates had to deal with the inner drive to be among those who made it, the pressure of playing the hero role in one's family, parish, and circle of friends, and the fear of letting everyone down. For today's seminarians, being one of the few seeking ordination in a society that devalues it carries its own anxiety.

Seminaries used to have very little unstructured time, but that is different now, and, once one has graduated and been ordained, parish work provides hours, days, and weeks of it. While some very motivated pastors may spend more than forty hours per week in direct, personal ministry and even add prison ministry or work with the homeless to a full week of parish duties, there is very little that a less motivated pastor *must* do apart from Sunday morning services.

While the need for perfection and control and too much discretionary time provide an environment for the development of a sexual addiction, the amount of negative attention focused on sexuality is another contributing factor. The more deeply one is involved in church, the more likely one is to have grown up with a negative attitude toward sex along with a prohibition against any mention of it. "The moralistic church, in its battle to control the lust-driven sinner, shares a common element with the addict: obsession" (Carnes, *Contrary to Love*, 89).

For seminarians of my generation and before, at the time when it was age-appropriate to begin to discover how one relates to the rest of the world as male or female, sexuality in the broadest and most integrated sense, sex in the seminary was perceived as isolated acts that were to be avoided. But the more one focuses attention on something that one wants but ought not have, the more one becomes preoccupied with it. And preoccupation is a part of the cycle of addictive behavior.

At the age it was appropriate for young adults to be learning to relate more intimately with others, Catholic seminarians were cautioned to keep their distance from women lest they "lose their vocation" and to avoid close friendships with fellow students lest they be thought homosexual. Students had been dismissed for both causes, and so it was an unwritten rule that any sexual thoughts or tendencies of any sort need to be kept hidden. The need for secrecy promoted hiding, covering up, lying, burying one's real self and projecting a false self, and it increased the isolation from others. Any system that promotes isolation promotes addictive and codependent behavior. If sex is a secret world the whole system refuses to deal with, sex can easily become the secret "place" where one goes to escape problems or the "drug of choice" one seeks to anesthetize them.

The more the problems mount, the more time one has on one's hands, and the fewer healthy outlets one has, the more time one can invest in one's "secret place" of fantasies and acting out. The more time one spends there, the more one distances oneself from others who might suspect, or others who might intrude on this very precious time. The addiction begins in emotional isolation and adds to it. Addiction covers poor self esteem, but erodes it further.

In the black-and-white thinking of a sex-obsessed church, there are only two choices: either one is virtuous and pure and "giving all" to God, or one is soiled by sexual activity and, in some way, holding back from God. That is still the message to the young seminary student, that he is called to be one of God's own, to work in the vineyard, and a pledge of celibacy is required to answer that call.

The emphasis on avoidance does not prevent sexual addiction; in fact, it contributes to it. "Those addicts who subscribe to the narrow model of good versus evil — essentially a model built on shame and control — may ... become not only pillars of the church but avenging angels out to destroy all lust.... Their crusades mean that they have only switched sides in the battle — not the foundations of their beliefs" (Carnes, *Contrary to Love*, 89–90).

Breaking the Cycle

Some church leaders, particularly in the Roman church, either have no experience of sexual love or cannot afford to speak to the members from their own experience because that must remain hidden, and so must address the issues with the disembodied logic that starts with, and identifies with, Augustine's personal disgust with his own physical-emotional self. It also means, in all denominations, that they cannot get help if they are in trouble.

Codependence perpetuates itself. In the present system, those with open, committed sexual relationships are not allowed to contribute to the institutional policy. And those who are policy makers continue to pretend to be celibate or to have no problems with that requirement; they continue the official attitude of disdain. There is no possibility of integration if we allow this dichotomy to continue. The official denigration of faithful love, sexually expressed, and the cover-up of clandestine sexual activity will continue until and unless those of us who have managed to integrate sexuality and spirituality, and who live those commitments openly, finally begin to articulate the profoundly spiritual dimension of those unions and to take the lead in writing and speaking on sexual sacramentality and ethics.

Codependence perpetuates itself. It is only in stepping out of our codependence, in claiming our right to know what we know and feel what we feel, and to speak what we know is right, that we can introduce sanity to this tangle of obsession and victimization.

6

Scapegoats: Bearers of
the Family's Displaced Disgust

A gay rights ordinance was up before Chicago city council not too long ago; a timely letter from the Catholic archbishop's office killed it.

The ordinance would have prevented discrimination in hiring or housing on the basis of sexual orientation. The code of public morality would be more uniform, if it can be said that our culture has any such code. The kinds of sex-related cases that would call for removal of a heterosexual person — for being a public nuisance in an apartment building, taking indecent liberties at work, promiscuity — would be the same grounds for removal of a gay, no more, no less. But this equaling of standards must have been too threatening, must not have been punishing enough.

Most of us are evidently satisfied with, or at least go along with, a gay-straight double standard. People dare not appear so "unsophisticated" as to take offense at seduction or "recreational" sex as long as it involves a male and a female: there are singles bars and restaurants that are in business to facilitate it. We may not be comfortable with it, but we have managed to numb ourselves to sexual license, as long as the participants are straight.

We seem to go along with church statements on sex as well, though we may be quite uncomfortable with them when those statements maintain that sexual pleasure is sinful. We try not to analyze the issues too closely lest it cause us unrest. We simply tune out the pope and give tacit approval to the church position as well.

Rather than take issue with our co-workers or, God forbid, with our church, we pledge allegiance to both extremes. Appearing to agree with two contradictory values while truly espousing neither creates tremendous pressure and requires tremendous personal and communal energy. Talking about sex, not joking or telling dirty stories but serious conversation on the values involved, can make us very uncomfortable.

Sex is a guilt-laden issue in Christian groups. There is guilt that some of the societal irresponsibility is our fault because we do not speak up about it. There is guilt that we ourselves are at odds with the public doctrine of our church. And there is some underlying shame that we are not "pure, as God wishes," not virgins as were the saints, but that we are sexual beings. We as a church are terribly unsettled in our views about sex; we are full of negative emotions, and have no healthy forum in which to deal with them. What do we do with all that guilt and shame?

The ancient Hebrew people wiped their hands on the back of a goat, symbolically transferring their sins and their guilt to the animal. Then they would run the animal (and the sins) out of the camp into the desert, presumably to die. There are two parts of the process: transference of guilt to another and expulsion from the community of the one chosen to bear that guilt.

Family systems counselors point out that dysfunctional families "elect" one of their members to be their scapegoat. The process may be unconscious on everyone's part, it may even seem that one individual has chosen to play that role, but the whole system together determines it, and the dynamic is the same. The scapegoat manifests some trait, or the anger or pain, that the others fear in themselves. The scapegoat is chosen to bear the guilt of the system and becomes the target for all the free-floating dissatisfaction and criticism that their situation generates. The family can center their attention on this member, act as if this one is responsible for all the ills they feel, and try to find some relief for those bad feelings by venting their emotions on the scapegoat.

The role of the scapegoat in the dysfunctional family, then, is to provide a target for the blame, an excuse for the pain, and a distraction from the real work of dealing with the true source of the dysfunction.

The Christian family has also "elected" a scapegoat — gays and lesbians — to bear our own unresolved guilt about our sexuality. Consider: if the family myth about sex is true, we are all sinners. (Who is concentrating solely on procreation, as Augustine would have it?) What do we do with the blame we do not think we deserve? Lay it on the scapegoat. What do we do with the doubts, the discomfort, the guilt that we feel about sex in general, or our own in particular? Lay it on the scapegoat. We have no "permission" in our religious institutions to create a forum for the healthy analysis of sexual morality, no "permission" to draw on the experience of those in faithful sexual relationships, even married heterosexual ones. So instead of giving ourselves that permission, instead of taking the initiative and using our energy to create that forum, we expend our energy by rounding up the scapegoats and driving them out of the camp.

Hester Prynne, the main character in *The Scarlet Letter*, was the scapegoat for her town. The townspeople punished one person for the sins of the many. And they did it with a vengeance, thankful that *they* were not on the receiving end. The gay community wears the Scarlet Letter for all the sexual guilt in Christendom.

Gay Identity in a Codependent Church

According to many evangelical churches, gays and lesbians are the devil incarnate, totally without principle, roaming around ready to devour children and unsuspecting adults. Catholic leaders describe them as people who are "intrinsically disordered." Such church rhetoric gives rise to and is supported by disturbing innuendos about what might happen to a community if gays were allowed to live or work there and inflammatory remarks about what "cannot be helped" if the majority decides to vent their disgust at these "rejects." Statements like these are seeds planted by otherwise decent Christian people, seeds that sprout violence with public approval.

Some Christian individuals, on the other hand, have discovered quite by accident that gays and lesbians are humans like the rest of us, and that their new friends have none of the idiosyncrasies portrayed in gay jokes. People with whom we share cordial conversations at work, in the supermarket, or at church, may be gay or lesbian, as might business colleagues, architects, government workers, attorneys, electricians, and construction workers. They are our sisters and brothers, cousins and uncles and aunts, and even our parents. (Some gays married in good faith and had children before coming to grips with their true sexual orientation. Some have adopted children.) Some are our mentors and our teachers.

Codependents fashion their public selves and make their choices to please others. We have all modeled ourselves on the standards projected by our home and church families. We have probably, at some point and on some level, bought into the established norm in our church family. Even if we do not agree with that norm, we have probably tried to live discreetly so as not to call attention to any actions or opinions that may deviate from it. We can be cordial at church, but choose not to talk about our ideas or actions. (Christians who disagree with the party line on sexual ethics are more likely to disagree in silence than to disagree openly; it is part of our codependence.)

As gay Christians in this codependent family grow in their own awareness of themselves, they have to deal with the horror that they might be one of those persons their church family has defined as evil and an outsider. To the extent that they have learned to accept that standard, they find that they are the enemies of their churches and enemies of their very selves. If they continue to go to church at all, they must take care to hide who they really are.

Codependence makes everyone victims. None of us escapes damage in this kind of family. But lesbians and gays, in particular, have been abused by this system that defines their very selves as beneath us. This abuse is similar to the dynamic we have seen too many times in our national history wherein we have labeled some group as less than ourselves, less than human — redskins, savages, niggers, krauts, gooks — and taken that label as permission to vent any pent-up hostility, to inflict any manner of cruel treatment.

The corporate policies of Christian churches make scapegoats of the gays. In evangelical churches, someone discovered to be gay may be asked to leave the congregation and almost certainly will be drummed out of the ministry. In the Catholic church, leaders treat gays with abhorrence and disdain. The inference is that this is one group God did not create. The best solution would be that they should cease to exist; the next best, that they should disappear.

The Christian corporate policy on gays actually drives them into the scapegoat role, actually encourages promiscuous behavior. Fidelity, which would involve being seen consistently with one other person of the same sex, may reveal one's orientation and expose one to harassment or physical danger at the hands of righteous Christians. Gays who do live in faithful relationships, and there are couples who have been together twenty-five years and more, cannot participate in church and community projects as couples. Faithful love is difficult, straight or gay, but since these relationships must be kept hidden, gay partners are cut off from any community to support and celebrate their fidelity.

Our theology has for a long time had a problem integrating individual acts of sexual union with the relationship they express. It has been a major problem for straight married couples for generations. The church has avoided the question of sex-as-expression-of-relationship by shifting the whole focus to procreation. That approach has not worked for straight couples, and it certainly does not work for gays. Gays are counseled in confession that they can be forgiven for isolated sexual acts, random couplings with strangers, but not for a long-term committed love, because that indicates a "state of sin," an ongoing situation of alienation from God. This makes as much sense to gay couples and their straight friends who have shared their love, as does the church "wisdom" that says any husband who approaches his wife with passion has reduced her to the role of a common harlot.

The most recent work of ecclesiastical abuse is the banning of gay meetings from church property. It is retaliation for gays asserting the right to speak for themselves.

The corporate policies of the Christian churches have kept lesbians and gays in isolation and fear of disclosure and have hindered the development of stable relationships. The very policies that scapegoat the gays, that displace onto them all our own sexual doubts and fears and try to relieve all those doubts by driving them out of our camp, have themselves fostered and promoted a lifestyle that is irresponsible and promiscuous.

The Gay Cleric — Codependence and Identity

One indication that church policy is a matter of displacing inner doubts is that a significant number of our priests and our bishops, some who are very dedicated to eliminating gays, are themselves noncelibate gay men.

"Gay priests are our own worst enemies," said a gay Catholic. "Many keep their own gay lifestyle hidden, but take part in the official condemnation of the rest of us, or at least stand in silence in their Roman collars."

Those gay priests who do try to carry church ministry to their own people face censure by the bishops. Some bishops simply admonish them and ask them to stop. Other bishops have gone farther and let it be known that they will revoke the "faculties," the right to perform official functions, of any priest who decides to minister to gays.

This universal condemnation and banning are scandalous, given the number of gay clergy and bishops in the church. While bishops are putting political pressure on aldermen, insisting that they vote against the rights of gays to hold jobs or live in apartments, they themselves have many gays on their own staff and payroll, living in their rectories and monasteries and seminaries, and looking back at them every morning from their mirrors.

All codependents are caught between two identities, the person whom others want them to be, tell them to be, or hint that they should be, and their true selves with their own ideas and feelings. This is true of any of us whose relationship with church is codependent, it is true of many gays who have not comfortably owned their identity, and it is true of many clerics who have sacrificed their true identities on the altar. Those who are clerics and gay besides may be using an identity rented from the institution to avoid having anyone see their real selves. The more they need to hide their real selves, the more determined they will be to pay the price on that rented identity, however expensive that might be.

If heterosexuality is the policy to which they must pledge allegiance, what happens if they are gay? They go underground. If celibacy is the required outer role, the public self, what happens to emotional needs? They get buried. Or they are released only in secret "other lives."

The consequences of any kind of open self-disclosure are too great: beyond the social stigma is the more powerful church rejection, and with that, the loss of their rented self, their public role or office. We are all the "bad guys" here, and all the victims. We, clergy and lay, have defined the physical as sinful and then spent time and energy trying to root out all traces of that sin, scapegoating the gays and insisting that our leaders stay "holy" and avoid all sexual activity. So gay priests have to keep that public image pure — by wearing a Roman collar and hiding the evidence.

The task of hiding a gay lifestyle is not as difficult for gay priests as it is for heterosexual priests who lead double lives. Catholic priests, at least, are expected to shun women, to keep company with other men, and to get away with their buddies for vacations and days off. It is not difficult to maintain gay relationships right in the rectory without attracting notice. But there is a duplicity involved, a deceit that takes away from true ministry, precludes any transparency or intimacy with the parish community, and must erode self-esteem.

Gay clergy live both sides — the scorning and the scorned. Many are too attached to the institution to risk a breach in that relationship by coming out. Therefore, they contribute to the attitude of scorn by wearing the uniform of a homophobic institution. Some will go farther, perhaps to divert public suspicion, by actively campaigning against homosexuality, bringing church pressure to bear on any individual or organization that is gay or ministers to gays.

Some gay clergy see themselves as victimized by the institution. This is a difficult perspective for the nonordained to understand; it seems to lay people that the clergy have the power. How could they be victims? James Wolf, in his book *Gay Priests*, gives insight into these clerics who have had to come to terms with their own sexual orientation in the condemning atmosphere of the seminary, who saw classmates dismissed for mere suspicion of being gay, and who have had to live with the harsh decrees of closet-gay superiors. Some have concluded, as have many straight priests, that the church has no right to impose celibacy, and that, therefore, they have no obligation to live it. They choose a close stable relationship for all the same reasons a straight person would do and try to put care and commitment into their ministry.

William Hart McNichols, a Catholic cleric, writes that "it is my experience that men, straight and gay, are programmed from early childhood to be object-oriented toward sex. There is great pressure to conform to the male view of sex, which separates sexuality from love and relationship and focuses on body types and parts. The male church focuses on sexuality in ways that are clearly foreign to the gospel." "Perhaps," he suggests, "gay priests could begin *from within* to heal the male church and the male culture of its broken sexuality" ("A Priest Forever," in *Homosexuality in the Priesthood and Religious Life*, 122; emphasis added).

Codependence and Recovery

The gay community reached a point in its own self-understanding from which the all-gays-are-aliens tone of the church documents no longer made sense. There was a moment of choice: to go along passively, take the abuse, and keep the "peace," or to take action. They took action and have continued to take well thought out steps out of codependence.

If being gay is itself an offense and gays must hide who they are or risk harassment, then it is difficult to find places where they can comfortably meet with friends, discuss politics or art or religion, and at the same time be themselves; the only places where they can relax and socialize are gay bars and other sex-oriented milieux. Gay Christians have created for themselves social contexts in which they can form friendships without hiding their identities. Dignity is one such national organization, with a membership of gay Catholics and with chapters in many cities. They meet for worship, fellowship, support, and the business of asserting their right to exist in a predominantly heterosexual church.

When the Vatican issued a patronizing and heavy-handed letter on the "pastoral care" of homosexuals, Dignity did not receive it in silence. They had meetings, reflected, and issued their own theology of sexuality, grounded not in Augustine, but in their own lived experience, integrating faith with life: "We believe that gay men and lesbian women can express their sexuality in a manner that is consonant with Christ's teaching. We believe that we can express our sexuality physically in a unitive manner that is loving, life-giving and life-affirming. We believe that all sexuality should be exercised in an ethically responsible and unselfish way" (Statement of Position and Purpose, adopted 1971, revised 1981 and 1989, Dignity/USA).

They are trusting more in their own thoughts and feelings, are willing to take responsibility, and are insisting that church officials also act responsibly. One of the hottest issues in Dignity right now is what to do with bishops who are so anti-gay publicly, yet are themselves non-celibate gays. Some favor "outing" them, making public disclosure of their orientation, not to imply that being gay is in itself bad — because for most it is more a fact of life than a choice — but to expose the dishonesty and cruelty from which these bishops operate. It is a delicate matter, but whatever the choice, it will no longer be guided by codependence.

The Lutheran church accepts gay candidates for ordination, provided they make a vow of celibacy, a vow not required of heterosexual clergy. Early in 1990, however, three candidates challenged that. They had successfully completed seminary and were ready for ordination. The man said he would no longer promise to live alone, and his approval was rescinded. The two women announced that they had had a covenanted relationship with each other and planned to continue living together. All three were called to churches in the gay community in San Francisco. The Lutheran church leadership was working full time to prepare a public rebuttal to the gays' claim to the right to be ordained. The church maintained that it had the right to describe and order itself, to say what qualifications are required for ordination. But that did not explain why gays could not be ordained. Then they said that the gays are not qualified candidates. But why not? Christian churches of many denominations invest time, money, energy — all resources that could be used in ministry, to make the point that the church still has power and to assert that gays are still outsiders.

The three new pastors, nevertheless, boldly stepped out of the codependence that holds back many more, declared openly their orientation, and made public their commitments to live faithfully with one partner and to serve faithfully the members of their church.

Some of us have had enough experiences with gays to know that they are persons and that the church condemnation of them is inaccurate and immoral. To the extent that we contribute to that official attitude or condone it by our silence, we are allowing the institution to supersede our own conscience rather than risk a rift in that relationship. That is a clear sign of our own addiction, our own codependence.

We are codependent, or part of an addictive family, in that we accept the scapegoats and add to the abuse. And even as we come to learn differently, most of us are very hesitant to speak, to say so, for fear of what others will think of us. It is very difficult to speak out in a group, whether you know those present or not, in support of the rights of gay and lesbian persons to live by the same rules as the rest of us. But it is a step we must take to get out of our own codependence.

Other Scapegoats

There are other scapegoats — those who display anything with which we are uncomfortable. "Silenced theologians" are an interesting phenomenon. If one indexed the topics on which they have written, it would be a good indicator of areas where church officials feel vulnerable. How does the dysfunctional family deal with uncomfortable topics? Refuse to talk about them. Refuse to allow anyone else to talk about them. Galileo was silenced — for saying that the earth revolves around the sun — by the same committee, the Congregation for the Doctrine of the Faith in Rome, formerly known as the Inquisition, that watches for "unspeakable" ideas today.

What is more interesting, I think, is how many theologians do not teach for the period of their silencing. They use the time for writing their next book, so the time is not completely wasted, but what does it say to the rest of the codependent system when the best and the brightest comply with these orders? It is time more said to their inquisitors, "I will talk with you about this if you wish, but I will not stop saying what I believe is true."

Divorced Christians have been scapegoated — made to carry the burden of the whole community's guilt and excluded from church life and activities because of that collective guilt. It is not possible to generalize here and certainly there is individual responsibility when a marriage dies, but, as was discussed in chapter 4, "The Rape of Marriage," the entire church institution has failed in its responsibility to live a mutually supportive, mutually accountable covenant. To try to rid ourselves of the problem by ignoring or victimizing divorced church members only reinforces our denial of our own problem.

Another type of scapegoating that is very common is the parish-level blaming for the state of the church. Clergy gather with their colleagues and decry the apathy and inactivity and stinginess of the parishioners. Church members will shake their heads at what "Father" or "Pastor" is doing or not doing that is ruining their church. Each side blames the other for what is wrong with the church, but neither side seems able to see that we are all baptized and all responsible. Neither side seems willing enough to take responsibility, to do all that they can do to change, to be church, to move in the direction of wholeness.

Toward Integrating Sexuality

The understanding that outlawed homosexuality in ancient Judaism also considered virginity abnormal: sex is for making family. Producing heirs was a duty to tribe and nation to keep control of the land.

The understanding that Augustine endorsed and that has dominated church thinking until now considers pleasure an aberration: sex is for making family. The reaction to the Vatican ruling on birth control has made it clear that the majority of Catholic married couples agree that, in their committed relationships, lovemaking is a right and a responsibility — for mutual pleasuring and to express their love, commitment, and gift of selves — regardless of their decision about conceiving. Couples in most other denominations seem to have come to this earlier and with less struggle. Sex is not just for physical reproduction.

Sex if for making family. This was the reason given for isolating gay men and lesbian women, but, if rethought, this understanding can lead to more acceptance.

Sex is for making family: it is a sacrament that both gives expression to and reenforces the covenant commitment. Lovemaking is the covenant feast that celebrates the commitment of two mature persons to be family to one another and to extend their love to bring others into their family embrace as well.

Eucharist is the lovemaking of the Christian community, and it is time it were more a sacrament of what we share than what divides us.

Part III

The Abuse of Power

7

The Only Franchise on God

The European settling of parts of the Americas brought into conflict two fundamentally different views of ownership. Many Native
Americans understood that the land belongs to the Great Spirit and that
humans are to share God's plenty and use it respectfully. The Europeans
believed that one could own the land, could put a fence around a plot
and say, "This is mine." I do not know what our culture would be like
today if we had adopted the tradition of common ownership. But I do
know that, for want of our understanding any of that wisdom, we have
subjugated and decimated the native peoples and continue to rape and
pillage the land. In the name of establishing civilization in a "primitive"
land, we have committed acts of insanity.

In the area of religion, the living out of our understanding of God,
there is a similar point of disagreement between those who believe that
God reaches out to all and is accessible to all, and those who believe in
"private ownership" of God. In the Judeo-Christian tradition, the stories
of the golden calf and the building of the Temple both demonstrate a
desire to hold and own God, to be able to say that God is *here* in our
possession, and all must go through us to get to God. That desire to
possess God existed in tension with the view that one must never try to
confine God to an image or building.

The tension continues in Christianity. Jesus lived very simply; he had
"nowhere to lay his head" and communed with God in his heart, in quiet
desert places. Yet some feel and teach that it is only within the walls of
church buildings, only within the auspices of church jurisdiction, that we
can reach God. The pope, who claims to be the current representative
of Jesus, needs a palace with guards, an international bank, his own
city-state, and a world-class art museum for official visits with God. We
build our edifices and our religious empires; we appoint magistrates to

administer the empires. And we say, "the one true God is only here in our temple, protected by our walls."

In the name of religion, we have committed another act of insanity. We have claimed to have the only franchise on God. This underlies all other claims made by closed and rigid Christian denominations. And what keeps members and leaders of those denominations inside the walls and under control, protecting and repressing more than planting and encouraging, complaining and protesting but not acting and not leaving, is that, on some level, they all believe that claim.

Even those who are enlightened enough to grant that outsiders can get a bit of God's mercy do not seem quite sure that they would get any of that precious stuff themselves if they were to leave the womb of their mother-institution.

God Is Wherever the Wind Blows

The Incarnation is a different kind of model. God planted a seed, and a dandelion, a wildflower, came up outside the wall of the temple, outside the circle of the religious elite. The dandelion stated, in a quiet and eloquent way, that God's love is manifest in the simple and the ordinary. Jesus' words were like the free-floating seeds of the dandelion, which took root in many other ordinary places, seeds that sprouted and blossomed and said, in the same quiet, eloquent way: God's love is manifest in the simple and the ordinary.

God's presence cannot be confined like a treasure in a temple, holiness guarded and walled off from the ordinary. The wild extravagance of nature suggests, and Jesus' life and teaching make explicit, that God would not choose to hide in one place, with access tightly controlled, but that God's presence is more like a dandelion, which scatters seeds in a most indiscriminate manner, which will sprout nearly anywhere, and which speaks not with might but with quiet eloquence.

If God scatters holiness and presence like the fuzzy, airborne seeds of the dandelion, then there is much more freedom in our relationship with God than we have yet seen, much more room to respond creatively, and much more responsibility on the part of every person to make the choices to do so. But freedom is threatening to a closed and rigid system. The closed-system response is to try to minimize freedom and personal responsibility, to put a mark of ownership on all the dandelion seeds, and to control where they might go. What a picture! Cages cover all the dandelions in a field, there are routing charts for all the seeds, and supervisors uproot any plant that dares to sprout outside its designated area.

Even history had to be retold to appear to be the prototype of this highly controlled pattern. So, though Jesus was born outside the sanctuary and the priestly class of his "church," even though he resisted the power yearnings of his disciples, and even though his words germinated in many unofficial hearts, we retell the story to fit into our pattern. We, in our wisdom, have decided to construct another sanctuary around Jesus and to establish another priestly class to administer and guard it. According to one revised story, Jesus made the disciples the first Catholic priests, granted them immediate promotions to pope and bishops, and gave them the exclusive franchise on all telecommunications systems linking humankind and God.

Walls around the Temple

If God is reaching out to us from all over, those who want to assert that they have the only connecting link are going to have to do and say things to keep people from looking in other places, to keep them from recognizing God in other persons or events. If we claim we have the only franchise on God, then we are going to have to manipulate God's own self-disclosure and try to put blinders on human minds. To assert that God gave us the only franchise, we will have to make God appear to be under voluntary confinement in the holy of holies of our temple rather than out scattering seeds in an open field.

Rigid churches operate, as do any other addictive families, by manipulation and control, and they do so for the same reasons — family loyalty, protection, and keeping the family secret. We have rules that keep people in fixed powerful and powerless roles within the temple walls, and rules that keep them from asking or even thinking questions — all "for their own good."

The rules that have been used to teach generations how to be "good Christians" are rules that deaden the spirit, teach blind obedience, and guarantee continuation of the same sick pattern. They are the same rules that have been hurting families for many generations. These are the rules that Alice Miller calls "poisonous pedagogy":

1. *Adults are masters of the dependent child.* Clergy and other church officials are unquestionably masters of the "lay children." No one may question what the clergy or their staff decide, or what the leader says is the intent of the Bible story, or else they will lose God.

2. *Adults determine in a godlike fashion what is right and wrong.* Whatever any authority figure says, is right, and is to be obeyed. Miller points out how the officers who carried out the extermination policies of the Third Reich were raised by good Christian parents who taught them always to obey authority. In church families that claim to have the only franchise on God, the adult characters or authority figures not only determine what is right or wrong, but claim to know and speak for the mind of God. Who could possibly dispute that kind of authority?

3. *The child is held responsible for the anger of adults.* The child must behave in a way that avoids challenging or arousing emotion in the adult. This is very typical of addictive households. The adult who angered has the unquestionable right to take it out on the child. Bishops will not challenge the pope; lower clergy do not challenge bishops; church members only tell the clergy what they want to hear. If anyone upsets the "superior," all "dialogue" is over and it is unquestionably the "lower" person's fault.

4. *Parents must always be shielded.* The child must defend the parent's denial system by not seeing and not saying what the adult does not want to face. The child is, in effect, expected to parent the parent. The child's own problems are defined as trivial. Church loyalty says we must always defend the institution; the authority figures must know what they are doing, even if our own needs are not being met.

5. *The child's life-affirming feelings pose a threat to the autocratic parent.* Some church officials cannot "handle" any other ideas or feelings that widen the horizons of theological understanding, or challenge their area of control.

6. *The child's will must be "broken" as soon as possible.* In *For Your Own Good,* Alice Miller cites a number of torturous incidents that were used as means of "teaching" children that their will is evil, not to be trusted, and that, no matter what, the adult will always win. Sadly, too many otherwise good people — parents and teachers and clergy — cooperate in trying to break the children, or any adults who dare to question, because they believe that this code of their church comes ultimately from God. Gifted people, trying to use their gifts in ministry, have been black-

listed and vilified to "teach them" that subservience to the institution is more important than any ministry.

7. *All this must happen at a very early age so the child "won't notice" and will not be able to expose the adults.* By the time they are old enough to talk and be heard, they have already been completely indoctrinated by the system. Most of our adult "formation" programs make sure that indoctrination precedes the granting of power; then when the bishop says that they must defend the wall around the institution, they will obey.

Poisonous pedagogy is based on a parent-child model: the parent is powerful and right, the child needs to be beaten. In church, however, adults function as both parents and children, and so it is only with the consent of both groups of adults that the system can function as it does. In church especially, the powerless adults are not physically dependent on the powerful adults; there are other sources of employment. And so both are responsible that this dependence continues.

The rules of poisonous pedagogy are the rules of codependence. We are in a codependent bind with church, unable to move for fear of abandonment, unable to question a church that alone has the power to save us, because we believe that the institutional church has the only franchise on God and because we accept and even defend that the rules of poisonous pedagogy are the appropriate operating rules for church.

Defending the Franchise

I have seen good people shift their actions further and further away from their own values in response to orders or in the need to continue these rules. Some have turned away from the very work they had wanted to support because their pastor or bishop told them it called their loyalty into question.

Acting or not acting in a way that is contrary to one's own moral values, supporting the status quo even though we see it as wrong, in order to preserve our relationship with the institution, in order to continue to belong, is abusing power or enabling the abuse of power.

Some will say that black is white and white is black to defend their franchise. At a church-sponsored "think tank" on marriage to which professional theologians and "nonprofessional," lay church members involved in marriage ministry were invited, ideas were voiced that directly contradicted the rigid rules on sacrament and annulment. Before the meeting adjourned, a cleric announced that our discussions officially never happened. "No one must ever know what was said here: they would not understand." On the contrary, they *would* understand; they might no longer salute.

Catholic bishops in Nazi Germany signed an agreement with the Third Reich that provided protection for the church in exchange for withdrawal of the church from certain political activities. The bishops instructed their priests to look the other way rather than address abuses (see Walter Marieux, *The Persecution of the Church in Nazi Germany*, 14f, with thanks to Peter Schommer). When the church plays power games, then and now, all other priorities are forgotten. Power corrupts.

Each Christian denomination celebrates the Sabbath with its own balance of Scripture and ritual. In some, the Lord's Supper is a weekly event, a covenant meal in which the members enact the commitment and inner dynamic of their community. In Catholic communities, Eucharist has become a point of contention between those who would like to keep control of the franchise and those who would like more liberal franchising policies but think they have to wait for a single corporate agent to share the rights.

There are fewer and fewer male, "celibate," officially designated clergy. Some parishes are visited by such a person only occasionally. In response to this situation and in a gesture aimed more at maintaining control of the franchise than giving service, the bishops have approved a modified Sunday liturgy led by a member of the local community, with bread that was blessed a week or a month ahead of time when a circuit-riding cleric happened to be in town. The whole rite is simplified and some prayers eliminated, so that there can be no doubt that whoever is leading worship does not have "the power of the priesthood." Only a few can share the only franchise on God.

Sadly, many members believe the family myth and enable the dysfunction. Codependence is not due to lack of intelligence. There are intelligent people who can cite theological, psychological, and sociological reasons why it is essential that Eucharist be celebrated weekly within the local community. The same people point to the moral obligation of Rome to "share the power," but stop short of claiming their own moral obligation to act on what they believe.

We have been trained to think this way; it is so difficult, almost terrifying, to consider other scenarios, other options. Perhaps it would be easier to see the issue in another context. The people of India had been taught that the government had the only franchise on salt. The salt was made from sea water, which should have been free to anyone, but the Indians were paying the government whatever price it demanded for their salt. Under the leadership of Gandhi, the people rethought their subservience, concluded that God owned the ocean, and that anyone had the right to collect salt from the sea. It cost them dearly at first to act on that new realization, but they did, and in so doing reclaimed their right to use God's ocean.

The gospel says clearly, "When two or three are gathered in my name, I am there." Concerning the weekly Sabbath supper and passover remembrance, it states simply, "Whenever you do this, do this in my memory." It is all the permission we need. There is a clear mandate. Eucharist was never really confined in the first place, but the story has been manipulated to seem as if it were addressed exclusively to a few. This is abuse of power. The rest of us go along with and enable the abuse: this is codependence.

Another way to defend the only franchise on God is to control the roster of church heroes and leaders. Besides the factors mentioned in "The Rape of Marriage" and above, there is another factor that keeps the "adult-masters" on top: some religious communities invest hundreds of thousands of dollars and the full-time efforts of some of their personnel into lobbying for the canonization of their founders or other significant members. They send out letters and prayer cards, collect miracle stories as evidence of sanctity, and solicit large donations to be used in both the canonization process and in building shrines to their "family hero." The benefactors who donate to these causes feel comfortable that they, along with the religious order, "own" a saint. I suspect that efforts of this nature would be repudiated by the very persons in whose honor they are done. It is abuse of power, aimed at keeping control of the franchise in the hands of a few.

Money Is Power

The institutional parent, or franchise holder, has the power to make certain decisions because it has the money to fund those choices. Where does the money come from? You and me. Television preachers have their big tin boxes; dioceses do too.

Funds donated to popular evangelical preachers have padded bank accounts, bought mansions, mistresses, and amusement parks, and financed the rise and fall of politicians and underlings. But among the followers, there is only one franchise and there are no open records.

Where does the money come from? All parish property and bank accounts list the bishop of their diocese as the "corporation sole," the sole owner. Any money willed to parishes can end up in the big box downtown. The diocese can take regular assessments from parish accounts or require that parishes contribute a set amount to the diocesan newspaper or other funds. Some moneys come from real estate — the building or lot next door might belong to the diocese — and some funds are invested in shares of companies that manufacture items the use of which the church condemns. But there is only one franchise, and there are no open records.

Where does the money go? Some is spent to assist low-income parishes, but those parishes can be closed without local consent. Some is spent to underwrite low-interest loans for new building projects, but churches can be built for the glory of the pastor against the wishes of the people. Some money pays off jilted girlfriends, or pays judgments in paternity suits. Some pays for attorneys to defend pedophiles, and some buys the silence of the victims. It all works because there is only one franchise, and there are no open records.

Money is power, and bishops who are corporation sole of large, well-funded dioceses have a lot of political clout. They can send large donations to Rome to show their loyalty and to ensure their own rise in power. They can also ensure that only the "party line" is taught and that "unacceptable" faculty are barred from the seminaries and some universities; otherwise, funding stops. There is only one franchise, and there are no open records.

We say we believe that the Spirit of God is constantly renewing the churches with new life. Yet when that new life begins to emerge — a fresher, freer, healthier way of being church — it is pushed aside as a temptation. (What would they say if I subscribed to that?) Or it is rooted out and destroyed as a threat to "our way," "the right way," "the only way." The dandelions we are pulling up may be our best pictures of God.

8

"The Church Alone Has Power to Give Me Value"

O ne of the most important signs of codependence is looking to another to give validity to our thoughts, feelings, and needs, to give us value as persons. As codependents, we do not feel comfortable about owning opinions unless we hear from another person that there is "room" for that opinion, that she or he approves of it. Unity with this other person gives us worth, and we feel we must preserve that unity at all costs. All our thoughts have to be measured against some-one else's before they become actions. This is what Anne Wilson Schaef calls "external referencing."

I found a good picture of that lack of confidence at a high school jazz dance production. Overall, the program was delightful; the girls had put in hours of practice. But I began to notice one dancer who was always out of step. She did not appear in every number, but when she did, she was a distraction. Then I noticed what was ruining her timing: she was keeping her eye on the dancer next to her and was trying to follow the other girl. That is external referencing, and when we slip into codependent behavior, we do the same thing. That dancer lacked confidence in her own ability, and maybe she had reason to do so, but the remedy for that is more practice, not dancing with her head to the side.

Chicago is blessed with the Hubbard Street Dance Company, a pro-fessional jazz troupe that explodes with energy. They are wonderful to watch. But whether they are all doing the same step, or doing different moves that eventually connect with each other, they do not look over their shoulders and get out of step. They practice until the music moves inside them and their bodies respond instinctively. They know that they know what to do. That is internal referencing, internal locus of control, inner center of gravity. And the best part of it is that, since they are not worrying about what to do next, they can put passion into what they are doing.

External referencing means that church codependents cannot do anything without looking over their shoulders to see how the church will respond. Will they accept me or condemn me? Will they say I cannot do this anymore? It means never acting with quiet confidence, never putting all one's energy into one's work and into personal and community growth, but always looking elsewhere for approval. It means driving forward with only the help of the rear view mirror or the directions of someone in the back seat.

External referencing is what causes some congregations or whole denominations to stumble around looking confused or to be rigid and lifeless. Everyone is looking over their shoulders, up or down the line at someone else, for an indication of what is acceptable, looking for approval, looking for their own value. Often what they find is a person or group that is itself obsessed with something to which they are addicted, and often that drug is power.

Many of us grew up with the conviction that we ourselves are nothing and that following our own inner sense of direction would only lead us astray. This conviction was created in part by the preaching we heard from our religious institution and partly from our own inner lack of self worth. So if our value depends on being part of this organization, we must at all costs do that. The relationship defines who we are and gives us the only worth we think we have. It is an addictive relationship; we feel we must maintain that relationship to survive.

The Idol of Conformity

Some Christian communities have erected an idol called conformity and expect all members to bow to it. The god is addressed by different names in the fundamentalist Protestant and Roman Catholic camps.

In the camps of some Protestant denominations, the literal interpretation of the Bible reigns. Members are expected to pattern their own lives after the lives of the ancient Middle Eastern peoples; it is considered a sign of their obedience to God. Literal interpretation of the Bible lends support to other codependent patterns of behavior as well: denial of personhood to those defined as outsiders, degradation of women, blind obedience to all authority.

Poisonous pedagogy derives much support from the reading of Judeo-Christian Scriptures without regard to their historical contexts. Unfortunately, those most affected are those who most depend on church. Very few members of these denominations have enough sense of history to place these stories in their historical context, to begin to understand how very different the lifestyle in biblical times was from ours. To attempt to read our Scriptures now without regard to their historical and sociological contexts is to infer that God sanctions racism, slavery, and cruelty to anyone different from "us."

On the other hand, those who teach Scripture as an absolute, particularly the more educated and influential teachers, are not likely to regard those texts as applying absolutely to their own lives. Even the most rigid leaders are selective in their interpretations. I know of no one who preaches, "If your eye leads you into sin, pluck it out," with the same vigor as "Women, be subject to your husbands." If they were to follow such injunctions literally, some evangelists would be called to do public penance by undergoing a wallet-ectomy, or perhaps some other life-altering surgery. A friend told me of a case a few years ago: a man cut off his ear — I guess it had led him into sin — and went on to castrate himself. But he was a listener, not a teacher.

Instead of relying on the Bible, the Roman church places absolute, unquestioning reliance on ordained leaders as the source of all truth. The hierarchical structure was inherited in the fourth century from the dying Roman empire. We acquired this Roman treasure in installments until we had it all. Pyramidal in shape and political in function, the structure is said to funnel the word and will of God down to the people.

Whatever the pope says on faith and morals is taken by some as a direct quote from God. The pope appoints all bishops and shares some of his authority with them, as long as they agree with him. All priests pledge obedience to their bishop and receive their share of his authority, as long as they agree. Some call this system "creeping infallibility."

In either tradition, once we have identified the guarantor of our security, we must conform to that standard. We obey without question and without exception. Some churches state it quite openly: blind obedience is the highest virtue. To belong to that denomination or to continue in good standing, one must conform.

If we have no value ourselves and truly deserve to be abandoned by

God, if our inner worth and eternal salvation depend on being part of this organization, we must remain connected at all costs. Fear of losing that relationship becomes the dominant factor in our choices, and we become more and more codependent on the church. Loss of our inner selves is the price we pay for security.

One way of maintaining a "secure" relationship with someone is by belonging to, caring for, or being recognized by that other. Codependence is evident in church members who seem to hover around the members of the "inner circle," trying to be indispensably helpful to their clergy. The situation is analogous to that of the child who cannot do enough for a teacher. Their sense of personal value seems to derive from their ability to help this authority figure. This dependence is not bad, but sad in that it speaks of an inner emptiness.

Once one understands addictive family systems, one begins to notice those church members who "live at church," the same few who are heads, or at least members, of every major committee, who place church activities above every other commitment — the "family heroes" of the congregation. When one understands family systems, one has to wonder what it is in their homes or their memories that drives them. Is it easier to "be somebody" at church than at home? Does their busy-ness at church numb the pain of an alcoholic marriage? Are they trading one codependent situation for another?

Boundaries

Codependents have trouble with boundaries. It is difficult for us to have a clear concept of ourselves apart from, independent of, the person or system to which we are addicted. We are what the system says we are. If the bishop is appalled, I am appalled. If the system says I have no gifts worth sharing, then I have no gifts, or will wait for recognition before I use them.

Codependents will do anything just to remain part of the system, even if what they are doing is counterproductive, or worse, contrary to Christian values.

A few years ago, I attended a week-long conference of Catholic lay leaders. (I do not like the word "lay." The attendees were both professionally trained and recognized for their gifts in their communities; that should amount to "professional." "Lay" does not describe them as much as it reinforces a mentality of clericalism.) The conference was to conclude with the celebration of Eucharist, and a Catholic cleric who lived in the conference city was called in to preside. He was sensitive and informed, warm and affable, but was not part of the organization nor had he been attending the conference. His only purpose in being there was to lead a group of people who already were community in sharing a feast that celebrates community, but he did not know them. (I addressed the inappropriateness of the "hired presider" in my first book, *Birthing a Living Church*: "If grandpa cannot be there to carve the turkey, shall we call in Manpower?")

When this man introduced himself that morning, he tried to address that problem and smooth it over, but in doing so he demonstrated the boundary issues that contribute to it. He said, "It should really be one of you up here doing this, but our church is not there yet." Where was the boundary that defined "our church"; who was he including in the group that was "not there yet"? He was there, and so were many of the people hearing him. The church gathered for that morning meeting was there. They could have celebrated Eucharist in a way that honestly reflected their values: equality before God, "neither Jew nor Greek, slave nor free, male nor female." They could have truly reflected the communal nature of the Lord's supper. And there was enough liturgical awareness among that group to do it beautifully, prayerfully, and faithfully.

As codependents, we have trouble having any boundaries at all. We have trouble even knowing where to put them if we choose to claim them. Our lack of boundaries has deprived us of our ability to act. We were "there": aware of the rightness of a different set of roles. But the "papa" of the larger church family was blind to those possibilities, and so we claimed for ourselves the same blindness: "It should really be one of you up here doing this, but our church is not there yet." There was no sense of identity as autonomous persons, or as a functioning Christian community, apart from the identity of the big institution.

To take it even further, there was no sense of the identity of that institution beyond the walled-off views of some of its members. I intentionally do not say "beyond the views of its 'leaders,' " because that would reflect a codependent perception as well. Those with titles are not necessarily the leaders. To assume so keeps us stuck, waiting for change to come from "up there."

We show our boundary problems when we ask permission of people who do not even have the breadth of vision to understand the question, much less to give an approving answer. We are unclear about our boundaries when we try to explain a need for ministry to someone who knows less than we do about the issue, and then limit the ministries to their vision. We superimpose someone else's boundaries on our own every time we hand over our decisions to someone whose priority is power, both the power of the institution and his own rise to greater power within that institution. And we do all that when we limit church to institution, when we limit leadership to male celibates, and when we beg those who have stopped listening to change their minds so we may change our lives.

True leadership often comes from those who have no official position, but an inner conviction and sense of simple, godly priorities. Jesus was such a one. Those who attract public notice today, those who rise to positions of organizational power, are frequently those who are most addicted to the system. The price they must pay to achieve that power, is the surrender to someone else of their own personal boundaries or the right to have boundaries. Their reference point is their superior or the system, but the relationships have become so enmeshed that they are not even aware of losing their distinct individuality.

Ordination

There was a time when I attended ordinations, ceremonies in which candidates are "commissioned" to the Roman priesthood. They were always exciting: church dignitaries in their red robes and gold miters, a sea of clergy all in identical vestments, splendid liturgy, magnificent music, and some good friends who had finally achieved the goal of their years of study. The last of the series of friends and relatives was ordained years ago, so I had not attended one of these ceremonies in fifteen years, until last year.

In 1988, a friend was ordained a deacon, and I was invited to the event. It is much the same rite as for priests, only this time my perception was different. My entire understanding of church had evolved considerably over the decade and a half. I had, by this time, finished writing *Birthing a Living Church* and was ready to move into a postclerical church. I had some serious doubts about attending the ordination at all. But my friends, the deacon candidate and his wife, had shared their struggles with "formation for ministry," and we had had some good talks about all sides of these issues throughout the period of preparation. So to celebrate the achievement of his goal, I decided to attend.

I had a place in the back of the cathedral; the building itself is huge and regal and makes its own statement about church. The entry procession was stately: the cardinal in his kingly robes was preceded by men carrying swords. People walked in order according to how much power they had or would receive. And the wives of the deacon-candidates, who had no power, and would receive none, were graciously allowed to walk beside their husbands.

The ritual was long and resembled a feudal investiture to knighthood, as well as a *divestiture* of all personal boundaries. Again and again, the men were called forward to pledge obedience to their lord-bishop. They completed their pledge by lying prostrate on the floor at his feet; they left their boundaries there when they got up. They promised to obey the pastor they served in the bishop's place. They even promised that, should their wives die, they would not remarry but would belong more completely to the bishop. There was no doubt what their one and only point of reference would be from then on. I could see some coming back down the aisle with the same look that I saw, long ago in some late-night movie, on the faces of the young virgins who were going to have their throats slit and be thrown into the fire for the gods — so happy to be accepted for this honor. It was impressive, all right. I left.

I took a walk down the street from the cathedral to get back to my own sense of reality. I reentered the cathedral just in time to see the church officials present a token rose to the deacons' wives. These women had undergone the same rigorous screening the men had (both had to be accepted or he could not participate), they had taken all the same classes, done parish projects, completed all the work, but, alas!, they were not males and so did not have what it takes to be ordained. After their husbands had been given the signs of their official status in the church, these women received a rose and some sweet words about being helpmates.

It was appalling. The women had just watched their husbands "marry" the bishop, promise that the directives of the pastor or bishop would supersede whatever they as a couple might consider best for their parishes, and heard them pledge that should they lose this wife they would not let another get in the way of their ministry. (There had even been a special word of praise for those men who came to ordination "untrammeled" by wives!) The institutional church had just walked all over the boundaries of their marriages and paid them off with a rose. Worse yet, all but one of the women accepted.

Who Do You Say I Am?

When Jesus asked the disciples, "Who do you say I am?," he was asking to see how much they understood. As a healthy person, he already had a healthy sense of identity. But codependents have no sense of identity, cannot set boundaries that define their own ideas, feelings, or right to decide, and so look for someone else to set those boundaries and define them from the outside. Many women who ask that question of their ecclesiastical institutions are waiting to be assigned an identity.

Churches may tell women that they have no identity themselves, but derive their identity from playing a supportive role to husband, children, and pastor. In the chapter on marriage, we looked at the pattern of counseling women to "stand by your man" even when he is abusive, even when the women and children are at physical risk.

Because the operative assumptions of some church leaders are that women have only secondary identity, any women who do have an identity, who do not look over their shoulders but do differentiate themselves and define their positions, run the risk of being maligned or blacklisted by the male power-holders.

Good codependents can hang onto hope most tenaciously — in spite of all evidence, in spite of their own better judgment, in spite of the knowledge that things cannot get better if they continue in the present direction. We allow ourselves to be gullible because we are afraid of the responsibility of being right, afraid of the decision we would have to face, to take other action and possibly even to leave the relationship.

I see this failure to trust one's own perceptions most in the middle-management level of most religious organizations. These are professional church people — not all are clergy — who are close enough to the big decision-makers to know that things are not as they should be. They see the scheming and manipulating of people and facts, the decisions that are made for political reasons or personal or institutional greed, the blacklisting of good people who dare to rock the boat. They see enough to know that, at the governing level, the mission of this religious body, the mission to which they personally subscribed and pledged their lives, is being betrayed.

They cannot deal with this head-on because it is too overwhelming; if they faced it they could not stay. So they try not to look at their situation too closely, hoping that God will make things change, that if they continue to work to keep this group going maybe some new leaders will come along who will be more devoted to the mission. Some of them even tell themselves that they, if they work hard enough and demonstrate their fidelity to the "church," will work their way into those decision-making positions themselves, and then they will turn things around and restore the original purpose of the group. But that never works. No one ever practices to be a prophet by doing the dirty work for dishonest or unscrupulous people.

Codependence is the underlying dynamic of some who are "perfectly happy" with what the church provides, even though it never touches their real lives and never begins to heal the hurts there. They cannot trust their own perceptions enough to question church policies and practices. They only know they must belong, and therefore they never allow themselves the right to express a dissenting opinion. They must conform, but only superficial thought is ever involved. Their perceptions, after all, do not count, even to them.

These are people whose decisions must conform to what "the church" says, even when it goes against their experience and better judgment, even though a voice inside says, "This has got to be wrong!"

Gullibility

It is a wonder that, in spite of the greed and sexual misconduct of some TV evangelists, the donations continue to roll in. Imagine all the people watching in their living rooms who are willing to do without something to send in five or ten dollars. Why do they give their money to TV preachers who use it to feather their lavish nests or buy another limousine? True, some want to believe that someone has the answers to their problems, but others want to get a letter from that important preacher acknowledging how generously they have given to the "work of God."

Why do members of the mainline churches make such substantial donations to the most questionable church building projects, shrines to the pastors or to the glory of the denomination, rather than to someone who will care for the needy, probably even pray with them, and not make personal use of the funds?

Ordinary people see in the church extraordinary power to "make them somebody." Something about giving to "the work of the church" makes them feel special, makes them feel that God approves, gives them a worth they did not think they had before.

Donating for recognition is an honest but misguided attempt by some people to get from the church, the evangelist on TV or in the pulpit, the affirmation they need to be whole. It is generosity to an illusion. The illusion is fostered by people whose honesty we can only wonder at. I suppose it must be granted that at least some of those asking that the hearers or viewers dig deep in their hearts and pockets must think the cause is worthy, though they participate in the codependent system belief that the individual has no worth apart from this superperson or superorganization. Others asking for funds are in the addictive role, completely centered on themselves and expecting everyone else to be the same.

The following is a letter I received from a retreat house. It is a request for a donation and would have gone directly into the garbage if it were not for the blatant manipulation of Scripture and values. The sender obviously expected a gullible codependent to open the letter; instead a *recovering* codependent opened it and recognized the game. The names have been fictionalized. Note the external referencing here:

Dear Friend [I had had no dealings with this group. They found my name on a shared or purchased mailing list.]:

Do you believe in miracles? Well, they happen once in a while here at "Our Place." Do you remember the Gospel story where Jesus praised the widow for giving from what little she had?

Recently I received a donation from a 75-year-old widow who is trying to help her daughter raise three children after the father abandoned them. Her note says, "I take care of the house, chores, shopping, cooking, etc., also financially trying to save her home." She goes on to relate her own severe health problems and the sequence of tragedies that have fallen on the family.

This dedicated widow shared the heart-breaking details of one grandchild's serial surgeries to save a leg. "She never complains about the pain, always so grateful for any and everything we do for her. Won't you please pray for her?" *You bet we will!* [emphasis in the original letter].

I believe it's a miracle that this widow has so much love to power her sacrifice . . . love made doubly strong by faith. *Of course* God will bless her efforts. Prayer and the strength of the whole family will carry them through this trial.

Another miracle is her thoughtfulness in sending a gift to us at "Our Place" in the midst of her difficulties. That's way beyond the call of duty!

I need you to work a similar miracle. Your donation to "Our Place" makes it possible for us to continue the ministry that inspired and strengthened our widow-friend. We can't keep going without your help.

At the end of her letter, the widow added: "P.S. I will send more when I can." Please share her miracle and send something now to "Our Place." We at "Our Place" ask Jesus to bless you and those you love as He blessed the Gospel widow, especially as we all pause for Thanksgiving.

May the spirit of Christmas peace reign in your heart throughout the coming year.

God bless you,
Fred, Religious Person
Director

It is a classic! It pushes all the codependent buttons: guilt, diminished self-worth, gullibility, willingness to be manipulated, the need to be needed. The letter used the sad plight of the poor widow to appeal to the codependent's sensitivity to the problems of others, but notice that the donations would all go to "Our Place," which provides retreats and relaxation for priests, not financial assistance for the poor. The widow would not have received any of the donated money!

For all the concern implied in this plea, there is a minimum of personal attention given to most of the sad incoming letters and usually no involvement in the lives of the hurting people who write them. This is big business; it depends on volume. Someone opens the letters, records the names and the amount of the donations on a computer disk, and discards the letters. The computer prints one of the standard thank-you notes. The members of the communities may never know anything about the stories they received. They pray generically, "God bless all of our benefactors," and nod toward a pile of computer-printed lists.

The gospel story of the widow's mite carried with it an implied judgment against the temple officials who lived in comfort on those donations. Today's widow keeps the brothers and priests housed and fed in the hope that they will pray for her. Then they advertise her suffering so that others, too, will send them money.

For us, it is time we begin to pray with our neighbors, "unofficial" though we may be, and help bear the burdens, rather than pay someone else to send them a form letter. That would be a step out of our codependence.

For the brothers, perhaps it is time they to learn to "sew tents" to support themselves. Then, to show their gratitude to the widow for her prayers, they could stop by her place with a bag of groceries and maybe stay a few hours to help with the chores.

"Lay" Codependence

Even when we protest the way the system operates, we can exhibit our codependence. The codependent will do anything to stay in a relationship, because the relationship is who they are. It gives them identity and purpose, even if the purpose is changing the other. According to Patrick Carnes, if they are still judging, they are still there, still codependent. Protesters, to the extent that their work is to make someone else change, are codependent. They reach autonomy when they finally step past protest to prayerfully considered action, when they step past protest to being the church that should be.

One assault to wholeness, one invitation to codependence is the term "lay" Christian. In law or medicine, the term "lay" means the uninformed and incapable. In an active community of believers, it is out of place: there are many gifts but the same Spirit. The focus of the word "lay" is on a perceived lack, instead of what gifts we do have. The focus is on status, instead of affirming that everything we have can contribute to the community, to the ongoing ministry of Jesus, and is of value.

Why is the one who helps family members to be reconciled called "lay," when the one who cannot do that but can preach is "professional"? Why is the one who *can* preach but is not *allowed* to preach called "lay," while the one who cannot preach, but reads canned homilies to the congregation is called "professional" or "clerical," sometimes even "pastoral"? Why do we go along with that? It is part of our codependence.

In the early church, the *laos tou theou* meant the people of God, the *whole* people of God, all the baptized Christians. While we may now recognize in that perspective a discriminatory attitude toward people of other beliefs and may take steps to alter our behavior so that we do not continue that Christian condescension, we can see that that early period did not have the lay-clerical stratification we have now. All the baptized were expected to use their gifts in service; inactivity was reprimanded, not expected. Certainly there was special recognition given the disciples for their experiences of having traveled with Jesus, but they were not considered "priests." Only Jesus was priest, and that in a special, exclusive, once-and-for-all sense.

The elevation of clergy went hand-in-hand with the spirit of dualism. In the fourth century, there were suggestions that since the presbyters, or elders, were to lead the rite of Jesus' sacrifice on Sunday morning, they should refrain from engaging in sexual activity with their wives on Saturday night. Elders were still elected from within the membership of a particular community and still married, but we can see two changes from Christian community life in the first century: Eucharist was not the family supper of Jesus' family but the emphasis was rather on the sacrifice of Calvary, the ultimate temple sacrifice; and the elder was not part of a council discerning the direction for their community of neighbors, but rather the person designated to perform the cult sacrifice. The suggestion of Saturday-night abstinence was but a first step to set them aside as different from, above, holier than the rest of the community, like the Jewish cultic priesthood that the first-century church would not countenance.

Those of us who grew up Roman Catholic heard ourselves defined as second-class from the beginning. Members of many denominations may recognize the same pattern, depending on the relative codependence of their home congregations. There were those who were close to God — the pastors, ministers, priests, nuns — and then there were the rest of us.

If we grow up accepting these categories, there is a probability that we will be codependent. We are the ones who do not have worth; clergy are the ones who do have it. "Lay" people are the ignorant and incapable; "clergy" are the professionals, so we give our centers to them. We look over our shoulders at the nearest clerical reference point to see what we may think, feel, or do.

Make Me Somebody Special

What is it that makes us keep looking to the church for the confidence we lack? What is it that makes us think that if we have a certificate or a title from the institutional church, credentials that no one outside the "club" recognizes, that we are somehow endowed with the knowledge, the wisdom, the power, with whatever it takes, to make us more than we are. We fear to take our own initiative. Even when we see a problem, feel the need to act, and know how we would go about it, we are still afraid. We are afraid that others would not take us seriously. We do not even take ourselves seriously! Who am I? I am nobody! So we sign up and get our loyalty scrutinized (Did you ever cause any "trouble"? Did you ever question your pastor, the system, or the status quo?). We pass muster, go through the program, and collect our Good Housekeeping seal of approval.

I am not questioning classes that truly develop skills for service. But some programs seem to serve no other purpose than to run people through the gauntlet and remind them that they are doing whatever they are doing only with the permission of the one and only source of power. Something inside us says this program will not give us anything we did not have before and will just take us away from our families more nights, but another part of us says we dare not question, that we will be one of the few who have "what it takes" to serve.

It reminds me of what the children on our block used to do when I was little. There was the "in group," and if you wanted to be somebody you had to be part of that group. When you finally appeased them enough to be allowed in, the group would take you behind a garage and whisper the secret word, and that made you different, special, one of them. Even if there was a gnawing feeling of disappointment on hearing that word, that this was not as special as it was made out to be, that you did not feel any different from the way you did yesterday, you could not say so. You had, after all, finally arrived; how could you say, "This is nowhere." How can you say to the other children, the nonmembers, "Do not worry, we are no different from you; we only carry on to make you believe that we are." How could you say that and give up the illusion of being somebody special? It was pretense, but those who had it guarded it. Worth came from the gang. From the inside it seemed hollow sometimes, though there were times when others did look up to you, deferred to you, acted as if you were somebody special, asked what they could do to be one of you.

A couple who are friends of mine, who are both in Twelve Step programs and aware of the addictive traps in church, shared this with me: "He almost had a 'slip' [the AA term for starting to drink once recovery has begun]. He started thinking about becoming a deacon again." He joined in: "Well, I was thinking about starting some youth ministry." He saw a need and felt he could respond to that need, but something inside needed a title. We do that, many of us, often: we want the institution to say we are special, we are worthy, we have value, because they have the power to give us value and we do not have it ourselves.

We feel the need to be tapped on the shoulder with the regal sword before we do anything within the sphere of religious activity, and what is worse, we think that to really be of value we have to function within the sphere of institutionalized religious activity.

Little children like to play where they can see their parent; they feel more secure. Only gradually, as they gain an inner sense of security, do they venture further away to play alone in the yard or at a friend's house. It does not occur to church codependents to start to play beyond the watchful eye of the parent-figure or to originate our own games that are not just emulating theirs. We are afraid, like the child is afraid. We are afraid that if we are not within reach of that parent, we will be abandoned. We are afraid, like the believers in a flat earth, that if we venture out on our own we will fall off the edge of the world. Our world is so small.

In our churches, a significant number of clergy are unable to trust their own perceptions: they act while looking over their shoulders for validation. They may look at the bishop — what will he think? — or at the pope, or at those members of the congregation who are most vocal in their dissatisfaction.

The elders in one Baptist congregation sat in the back of church during votes and did not raise their hands until they could see how their own family matriarchs and certain financially well situated members were voting.

Only when they check on what is acceptable with this "higher power," will they do or think or say what "the church" will allow. Some will object to this criticism: "Of course they look around first; their job is on the line." That is true, very true, and that is one of the best reasons to move away from the prevalent model of church in which the clerical role is both a full-time occupation that affords one's food and shelter and a major source of status: it breeds a codependent clergy.

Since so many look up the line for more authority, it might be interesting to consider this question: how much "authority" does one need to speak the truth? If the system teaches that the right to speak always comes from outside oneself and "up the line," then one can never have enough authority until one stands at the top of the line. We have bishops who feel they cannot teach the truth because Rome might take away the title that is their identity, the title that gives them their right to teach. It is a Catch-22. It is paralyzing. It is causing more decay in the institution.

Crowds listened to Jesus, and he did not have a halo, he did not have any credentials accepted in his religion or society. "His teaching made a deep impression on the people because he taught them with authority, unlike their own teachers" (Matt. 7:28–29). The truth has its own power.

9

The Big Lies and All the Little Lies

I used to think that people lied when they were backed into a corner, when they were afraid, when there was some benefit to be gained by lying, or when they had done something they did not want to admit to for some reason. Strangely, those kinds of lying made sense to me; I could see why people resorted to them. What I have since realized is that lying does not have to make sense. Addicts, people raised in addictive family systems, and co-dependents do not need a reason to lie. Frequently they do not know the difference between dishonesty and truth. (Anne Wilson Schaef, *When Society Becomes an Addict*, 53)

Sincere delusion is believing your own lies. The addicts who make a commitment to change or follow through on something are sincere in their intentions. They are as sincere as when they vow to themselves to quit. They may experience a great deal of emotion — tears of pain, expressions of tenderness, or anger when someone doesn't believe in their good intentions. However, their commitment to others is no more valid than their vows to themselves. It appears to be paradoxical to be sincere about telling a lie. It is not. But it is evidence of seriously impaired thinking. (Patrick Carnes, *Out of the Shadows*, 7)

Anne Wilson Schaef says that all addiction involves fundamental dishonesty — to oneself, to others, and to the world (Schaef, *When Society Becomes an Addict*, 51). Addicts lose touch with what they think or feel; the addictive substance or activity protects them from facing what is inside, and they become progressively less capable of honesty with themselves. They are dishonest with family and friends, lying about and covering up their addiction:

> In AA language the addict is a "con." We all know what con artists are: People who will cheat you, lie about themselves and/or the products they are representing, and take advantage of you at the earliest opportunity. Addicts are terrific cons. They are particularly good at figuring out what is appropriate, expected behavior and behaving that way, even when it has nothing to do with who or what they are. (*When Society Becomes an Addict*, 51)

Since addicts lie to their families, the family members become confused, become less able to trust their instincts, begin to lose touch with what they think or feel. Family members learn to live the lie the addict has created, to accept the addict's view of life as reality. So they all take part in the lie to the world, hiding the treatment they receive and projecting the image that they are successful and on top of things.

Codependence is an addiction, whether to an addict or to a relationship that gives one value, and so it too involves all three kinds of dishonesty.

"Denial" is a term used to describe the fundamental refusal to face the addiction and the unmanageability it has caused in one's life. Addicts are said to be "in denial" of their own compulsions and the impact of those behaviors on those around them. Family members can be in denial of that other person's addiction ("She only takes pills when she's under a lot of stress." "He is a good provider, so if he gets drunk or rages sometimes, we shouldn't mind.") And they are often in denial of their *own* compulsive activity, of their own codependence. ("I couldn't have her get all upset, so I cleaned it up." "He isn't ready to see things that way yet, so I'll wait.")

Therapists distinguish between denial and delusion. Denial is refusing to face the problem or its seriousness: lying, making excuses, refusing to talk about it. Delusion is *believing* one's own lies, so that the myth we tell others becomes reality for us.

In the case of church codependence, the three groups that create that addictive family system — the members, the clergy and other middle management personnel, and the top decision-makers — each participate in the lie. Some are addicted to power, are in denial about that addiction, create myths to rationalize or cover their addiction, and play the "con."

Others repeat the myths as facts, make excuses for whatever the myths do not cover, protect everyone from facing reality, and try to smooth over any adverse consequences of the dysfunctional behavior. And the people in the pews choose to suspend any doubt about discrepancies between the myths and reality, remain quiet when we experience abuse, and manage to convince ourselves, our children, and our neighbors that everything is fine here at home in the church.

Dishonesty and Denial of the Members

As church members who have given up our centers, we have cut ourselves off from our own perception of the truth. We are, as it were, driving drunk. We are driving ourselves, our children, and our church, with our minds in a warm haze. Can drunk drivers be prosecuted for what they did under the influence? Once we have disconnected our thoughts and feelings, are we the less responsible because we must now function without them?

We lie to ourselves that we are being nourished when we are not. We pretend we are happy with the menu, because to do otherwise would risk rupture of the relationship. We lie to ourselves to keep the inconsistencies and abuses of the system in that warm haze, to keep inadequate leadership in a blur. We do not want to see those things, so we do not "see" them and lie to ourselves to quiet the doubt. We lie to ourselves to cover our own codependence. We do not really want to face that we are working overtime to do the work and then praising the assigned leader for a job well done. We do not really want to face that much of our "niceness" is an attempt to control the decisions and behavior of the "more powerful" in the church, nor that most of our efforts at control are in vain. We do not really want to face that we are waiting for "them" to change when it is we who need to change. We lie because we do not want to face the facts, and we do not want to face the facts because we do not want to make the choice.

We members lie to others. We lie to the children in repeating doctrines we no longer hold, because to do otherwise would threaten our security. We lie to adult candidates coming into the church, or at least give them a false impression, by keeping secret our own doubts. Because we lie about the way things are and cover our true challenges and options, we teach and reinforce codependence as part of the "gospel" of Christianity.

The second group, clergy and other middle management, may be more caught in the lie because their lives are so wrapped up in the institution and because their identity comes from it. Some lie to themselves that they continue to be priests out of preference and not out of fear or addiction. As it becomes harder and harder to face the tough questions — is this lifestyle even healthy? — many drink, work, eat, or use sex to anesthetize the doubts. And then there are more lies to cover the addictions that are covering the primary addiction to church. Some deny how dissatisfied they are that they are not doing what they aspired to do, that their job is more financial governance than spiritual awakening, and that they are afraid to leave, to live without the system. They try to hide from their own codependence.

Middle management personnel lie to others in preaching what they themselves no longer believe is true. A member of a men's religious community became the superior of one of their houses when he was fifty. By that time he had recognized that his own early choice to enter that community was a mistake. He came to realize that the lifestyle was more harmful than helpful to him, and yet he told himself it was "too late to leave." He was afraid of facing life without the community. So he continued for twenty more years to train younger men in a lifestyle he wished he had never chosen, a lifestyle he thought was hazardous to anyone's emotional health. For twenty years he lived a lie to his colleagues and to the younger men who looked up to him. And for twenty years he told himself another lie — that he had no other choice.

It is a lie to hold up clerical or religious life to others on the outside as something to be sought when one does not honestly find it so. An acquaintance who does military recruiting explained how easy it is to lie about the life: "You just tell them the good stuff and leave out the bad." Clerical recruiters do the same: everyone will look up to you, you'll have the freedom to travel, be welcomed in every home in the parish, be treated to the best of food. The lie is in what they don't say: clerical morale is at an all-time low, addictive behaviors are rampant, the system is unresponsive, the loneliness is debilitating, and underneath it all is the fear that not only is the universal admiration not there, but many do not even care about what you are doing.

Clerical comments to the outside world, especially about something that might prove an embarrassment to the system, are couched in "churchspeak" and are designed to cover, distract, or reassure — anything but give a straight answer. Several years ago, "a decree went out from Caesar Augustus," the bishop of a diocese, that the "period of experimentation" was over and that all children in religion classes were to be taught to go to confession before they could be allowed to participate in communion. A woman involved in religious education called downtown to find out the reason for the change. Her inquiry was shuffled from one office to another; each middle management person would answer that the bishop said it was for "excellent pastoral reasons." When that answer was not enough — what are those excellent pastoral reasons? — the person would claim ignorance and transfer the call. "Sister Alice probably knows; one moment please." Finally, one cleric let down his guard: "There aren't any 'excellent pastoral reasons.' The bishop is paranoid because adults don't go to confession anymore, so he's insisting that we go back to making the kids start early. But if you ever quote me on this I'll deny it."

The policy went against what many teachers felt was the best interest of the children. Why didn't more teachers and pastors question it? Why weren't there a hundred calls for explanations?

Teachers and clerics continue to insist that the sacramental rituals are of primary importance to Christian living, even when they are tired of the vending-machine mentality and even though those events seem neither to express moments of growth nor bring about changes in the lives of the parishioners. The clearest example is confirmation. Long ago a part of baptism, confirmation was separated only to show some connectedness to the nearest bishop and to allow him time to make the trip. Given its history, some theologians and religious educators advocate returning confirmation to its original place with baptism, whether the candidate is an infant or an adult.

As a child, I was taught that confirmation made us "soldiers of Christ," strong enough to take on the nonbelievers in the world. As an adult I discovered that that rationale was based on some early medieval document that has since been uncovered as a fake. So we had to pound our swords into plowshares and look for another reason for the separate rite of confirmation.

Next to gain popularity was the notion that, since most were baptized as infants, we should make some commitment on our own to the church. But how independent are we at thirteen? There is a control issue here: an attempt to coerce loyalty while we still can, fear that if the young people get older and more independent they won't pledge at all. So we put them through the motions of pledging lifelong allegiance and throw in some other customs of dubious significance, like claiming a new name.

An eighth-grade boy in a local Catholic school was told he needed to select a saint's name for confirmation and began looking for information on "St. Genesius." He found the name mentioned in a "Batman" story as being the patron saint of comedians and jokers (the Joker character in the Batman movie is vicious and kills in cold blood for "fun," but seems to capture the gore-loving imagination of adolescent boys). The boy figured that if he had to take some saint's name, he would claim the patron saint of the Joker. Another lad in the same class looked for any name that sounded macho and started with a certain letter so his initials would spell his first name. Some eighth graders even felt that all confirmation meant was the end of parochial school or catechism class, that soon they would be free of religious education. Does this sound like they're involved in a process of personal commitment? Yet they will all be confirmed, ready or not, on whatever day the bishop's secretary has scheduled his visit, and the adult leaders and local clergy will sigh and be glad that they "got them committed" to the church. We are fooling ourselves and wasting the precious time we do have with the young.

Institutional Dishonesty

When we talk about dishonesty at the institutional level of the church, dishonesty becomes what psychologists call delusion: the people are so deep in their own lies that they cannot tell the difference between what is and what they say. They come to believe their own stories. At the decision-making levels of institutional Christianity, office holders seem to really believe that they alone have the power they claim, that they need to protect it at all costs from any who might threaten it, and that all the choices they have made or will make have God's seal of approval. Some, at least, truly believe that what is done to them is done to the church; what is done to the "vicar of Christ" (one of the titles claimed for the pope) is done to Christ himself. And, therefore, whatever they do to protect "God's chosen" from public censure is all for the good of the church and is a measure of their loyalty to God.

At the institutional level, we come face to face with the addiction that is at the heart of the church-family's codependence: the addiction to power. It is typical of all addiction in that communication — with oneself, with others, and with the world — becomes deceptive as a matter of habit, beyond reason or choice. For example, there are many cases of clergy traffic offenses, from speeding to drunk driving, that go unreported to "protect the good Father" and the reputation of the church. There are other more serious offenses that do not get anywhere in the legal system either: no one wants to touch a "tight collar" case. Obviously, police and civil authorities cooperate in this and probably consider themselves good church members for it. But when the archbishop of a large diocese had a heart attack, staff members closest to him wanted that kept quiet too; they did not want him to appear vulnerable. They had covered up so much for so long that manipulating the news had become policy.

Chapter 5 discussed the double lives led by some "men of the cloth" who have long-term or random sexual liaisons while continuing to appear celibate or faithfully married. When that kind of undercover behavior becomes rampant, when outsiders are hurt, it becomes increasingly difficult for church officials to keep the incidents out of the public eye. There is a high price to pay for that kind of silence, so high that protecting the image of celibacy or sexual propriety may be the largest item in some metropolitan church budgets.

A priest who fell in love with a woman and wanted to resign the priesthood to marry her met with his bishop to apply for a return to lay status. The bishop tried to talk him out of leaving the clergy by assuring him that, if he stayed (in the active, "celibate" priesthood), the diocese would "take care of the woman." The priest was disgusted. He told the bishop to save his money; he resigned his priesthood and married.

In a church whose policy on clerical celibacy is "get your needs met but keep it quiet," pay-offs are regularly used to protect the image of the church by keeping clerical indiscretions out of the press and out of court. Funds are paid under the table to pregnant girlfriends, former girlfriends who are mothers of priests' children, irate husbands of pastors' lovers, and, worst of all, to the parents of the child-victims of clerical pedophilia. Should one of these women or parents try to pursue justice in the courts, the game gets rougher.

The chief attorney for a diocese, a tough lawyer from a big firm that regularly handles cases for the church, told a meeting of priests: "In sex cases, we'll stand by you no matter what; we consider the family [of the

victim] as the enemy. We will protect you and get them to back down."
Very few families can afford the legal fees it would take to fight the kind
of clout that the church has.

How many cases of clerical pedophilia make the papers? Many more
are covered up. One young boy tried to tell his bishop what a priest
had done to him, but the bishop forbade him to say anything about it
to anyone else; and he was only one of many victims of that particular
priest. The families are intimidated, told they will never win in court,
and paid something on the side. The clerics are quietly moved to other
parishes across town — priests in treatment for this sort of thing would
look bad — where they are welcomed for being so friendly with the
children. Such a breach of trust!

Look at this from the other side. There is a noticeable lack of public
curiosity about these kinds of things: we do not want to know. The
more we know, the more responsible we are to make a choice about this
relationship, and we do not want to choose. The official cover-up fosters
codependency in the system, and the widespread codependency allows
the cover-up to continue.

Many of us are accustomed to the tooth-fairy method of arriving at
decisions on church policy: go through the ritual at the parish council
meeting at night and the decision appears magically in the morning.
Projects begin, buildings go up, parishes and schools close, personnel
appear and disappear. The real tooth fairy, the political machine downtown, would not be able to continue delivering these surprises if its
identity or methods were found out. So for its protection and our continued "benefit," the machine has two cardinal rules: protect the bishop
and leave no fingerprints.

The uncovering of the Iran-Contra arms scandal was an eye-opener
for many of us. How amazing that someone could have so much power
that his any wish, even an unspoken wish, could become a mission for
his loyal underlings. Yet it happens all the time much closer to home.
Some bishops make it known that they would rather have their assistants
do the dirty work without implicating them: "Do what you have to do,
but don't tell me."

In good-news events, the tooth fairy is always credited, but if the
news is bad or incriminating, someone else is set up as the responsible
party. Some decisions are officially said to have come from a parish committee, a committee of selected experts, or the bank, but the decision itself
came from downtown — the spoken or unspoken wish of the bishop,

the work of the machine. The reasons are explained in churchspeak, but the real reasons are known only by the machine.

The withholding or limiting of information is dishonest. The setting up of dummy committees to announce predetermined decisions is dishonest. Those who make the choices to conduct church business by those methods are living in their own delusion — God put me here, so whatever I do must be best for the people — and they are reinforcing the codependence of the system.

"The Doctor Will Be Right with You," and Other Deceptions

One afternoon I had to take one of my children to the doctor's office for a sports physical. On this occasion, I went to a clinic where we did not need an appointment, but where the wait was usually no worse than at any other medical facility. When we arrived, the nurse had us fill out some forms and showed us where to wait. We had waited forty-five minutes, long enough, I thought, for it to be our turn, when a man walked in from another office in that building. He had some kind of injury and wanted a doctor to look at it. I heard the nurse tell him that he might as well return to his office and come back later because there was no doctor in the clinic, and she did not know when one would be coming in. When the man left, the nurse went back to her business. She never gave that message to the rest of the people in the waiting room so that we could make our own choice to stay or come back another time. She left us all with the impression that in a matter of minutes the doctor would see us. It was a lie.

An institution that is addicted to power is no more likely to acknowledge that it cannot fix something than that nurse was to admit that there really was no doctor in the office.

Closed-system churches, either biblically or hierarchically based, tend to be major obstacles standing between addicts and treatment. The *Chicago Tribune* published a series on the Catholic and Pentecostal churches, in which they told a story of a Hispanic Catholic who went to confession to talk about his cocaine addiction and was told to say five Our Fathers and five Hail Marys. The Pentecostal church, on the other hand, welcomed him warmly and took him into a small room for church counseling (Jorge Casuso and Michael Hirsley, "Wrestling for Souls," January 8, 1990). While many find the Pentecostal churches warmer than the Catholic churches, neither one sent this man to Narcotics Anonymous. The temptation is to say: we have all you need right here; just pray more or go to confession or claim Jesus as your savior and your addiction will disappear.

The marriage annulment process was treated at length in chapter 4. It is another example of an institutional claim to be able to fix members' lives, though the process often fails to get at the root of the problem and does not follow through with counseling.

When a parish is in need of a new pastor, the diocesan clergy personnel board sends out a team to poll the members regarding the type of individual they are seeking. This is very impressive to someone who has not seen it done before; it makes the church appear to be so much more responsive than it was years ago. The board circulates questionnaires, holds a parish meeting, and assures the members that they will do their best to match their expectations. What they do not say is that there are so few clerics available anymore that they will be lucky to get a replacement of any description and that the more gifted ones are sometimes sent to more affluent parishes. The parish will get one of the two or three who are available, regardless of what they put on their wish list. One cannot ask a magician to pull a dove out of the hat if the hat contains only a rabbit.

While Catholics cannot fire a pastor, it is theoretically possible to bring one before a diocesan arbitration board to address grievances and work toward a resolution. Anyone who has an abundance of time and emotional energy they are willing to throw away should try it. This board does its own kind of magic, with waves and sparkles to distract audience attention while the man slips out of the box. They assign some of the best listeners they have, and those individuals spend many hours hearing the complaints. The hope is that that will be enough, that once the people feel they have been heard, they will be content and go home. If the parties persist, a different illusion is used; the case may be referred to a higher official with whom the process is repeated. The parishioners are kept busy until they tire of it, and then, it is hoped, they should go away. If one stays with the case all the way, one learns that the listeners have no voices. There is no power, just props. There is no real recourse. Sooner or later, the parties see what is happening and give up.

In spite of all the abuse, addictions, politicking, and power struggles that go on in the church, the diocesan newspapers, like *Pravda*, print only the news the people "should" know: which parish is having a bazaar, who has been a religious sister for fifty years, which priests have died.

Institutional dishonesty creates a false self for public display, while the real self is kept behind closed doors. This is not the same as, say, parents who may listen to their young children, discuss the matter privately with each other, and then present their final decision. A parental decision involves those two — it is both their right and their responsibility — and most parents now at least discuss the reasons with the children and often involve the children in decisions that affect them. But church decisions should regularly be made by *all* those who are active contributing members, or by their freely chosen representatives.

Church members are not children; we are the ones who pay the electric and heating bills, who fund the expense accounts and underwrite the airfares to Rome. However, if church members are codependent, we are, by our own choice and habit, relating as children in this system. We are, by our own choice and habit, codependent on church and in denial of our own addiction, and we will remain addicted until we admit it and take steps to recover.

Circular Thinking

While the party line is that celibacy is necessary because it leaves ministers free to devote all their time and energy to caring for God's people, in fact, it costs money and personnel time and clergy are less involved with the needs of the people so that they can "cope with the frustration" of having no (apparent) sexual partner. The vacation time (six weeks for some) is much more than most parishioners will ever get. And I don't remember a Catholic cleric using his vacation to paint the house. Yet the defense is, "anyone who has to give up a life of his own deserves a few extras." The price tag on restaurant dining, fine liquor, and vacation travel by many Catholic clergy is much heftier than for the married blue-collar workers who support them, at the same time caring for children and making house payments. And yet, some of the people gladly contribute because "Father is giving up so much."

They have to be celibate to be more available to the people. They have to get away from the people and have more vacations and dinners to "sublimate" their celibacy.

The top decision-makers tell the people that priests must be sexually abstinent to "be there" for the people. The priests feel they have to be sexually involved to "be there" at all. When they do get involved sexually, the church pays the people's money to hire attorneys to cover it up because, they say, "the people would not understand if they knew." In the end, no one is there — open, honest, and available — for the people, and they are being used and deceived besides.

Addictive thinking is circular. It is dishonest and manipulative. It is a cover-up and a con. There is no communication of real information in either direction. No one is allowed to question, or to bring in outside information, because that would be disloyal. A closed system is its own defense. And in the church, the ultimate defender of the system is, supposedly, God.

10

Nailed to the Wrong Cross:
The Addictions of Religious
Codependence

I magine Jesus starting his ministry with the religious authorities of his "church": he makes an appointment, explains his vision, and points out how it echoes the message of the prophets, how it is consistent with their tradition. He asks permission to teach this vision as a way of life, which is, of course, denied. Now, imagine he accepts their decision, goes home and builds tables, and returns to Jerusalem every few years to make an impassioned plea before his church's "General Assembly" or "Curia." He retires from the religious arena except for an occasional vain attempt to change the system.

If Jesus had done that, he never would have fulfilled his mission to teach and heal and lead. He never would have attracted enough public attention to warrant the "bishops'" efforts to get him crucified either. But he could have consoled himself that he did try, that he was rejected, and, after all, he was suffering. Is that not a sign of God's favor?

I do not want to minimize the spiritual dimension of human suffering that can be discovered when we accept what comes our way, or when we incur suffering by extending ourselves for others. But it is also possible to use suffering as a substitute for mission. It is especially common for church codependents to tolerate or even to seek out suffering as a "properly holy" place to expend the energy that should be going other places.

The worst part of religious codependence is that we do, in Jesus' name, the very things that he shunned. We do those things with a martyr's mentality. And we do them repeatedly, compulsively, as if we had no choice; both our actions and our inner dynamic fit the pattern of addiction.

We are all on a mission from God. We have unique gifts and insights to share, personal energies to invest, in developing ourselves, our families, our communities, and our world. For us, as for Jesus, there is an inextricable link between our self-actualization and our mission. Seen from this perspective, codependence is an abdication. We put our calls and gifts into the hands of someone else, and then use our energy to try to get that other person to make good use of them. It is an exercise in futility, the kind of craziness and waste that is typical of addiction.

Jesus faced crucifixion rather than bow to religious power, rather than put man-made religious traditions ahead of God's law to care for others. We find ourselves doing just the opposite: wasting the gifts and opportunities for service we have been given, and enabling the power-greed of others, all the while claiming to be following Jesus' example. We are not, as we sometimes claim, being crucified by the church, or even by world: we are addicted. We have nailed ourselves to institutional religion with the nails of our own codependence.

Chapter 1 introduced the relationship between codependence and church, the core beliefs behind addictions, and how addiction and co-dependence are handed on from one generation to the next. Now we will take a sober look at the cycle, or inner dynamic, of addictions and at the negative consequences of addictive codependence in church. This is not to lay blame at anyone's feet: most of our predecessors only handed on to us what they received from others. But we need to recognize the sickness in order to begin to get better. There is the saying: "Those who ignore history are condemned to relive it." Those who continue in the denial of their own addiction not only condemn themselves to more destruction, but condemn their children to the same. Somebody has to begin to break the cycle.

The Addictive Cycle

The core beliefs give rise to a cycle of behaviors that puts the addiction into practice. Craig Nakken and Patrick Carnes both describe the cycle, and in very similar terms.

Nakken says the addictive cycle begins with pain, but for an addict this can include any negative emotion — fear, sorrow, frustration. Pain signals the urge to "act out," to do the addiction, whatever it is. For a food addict, any negative emotion activates feelings of hunger. For a nicotine addict, any uncomfortable emotion signals that it is time to light up. Compulsive shoppers under stress feel the need to head for the mall.

Addicts live with that urge, mentally pacing back and forth, or obsessing about what they want to do, until the tension reaches a point where they give in and shop or eat or gamble. The acting out provides momentary relief from the indecision (whether to act out or not) and from the original pain, but the relief is short-lived. Before long, relief is replaced by despair and more pain: despair that they have gone back on their word to themselves and "done it" once again, that they are out of control, that they have in some ways made things worse by doing this; and pain, the pain that they were trying to escape and that is still there after the binge, and the pain of lowered self-worth.

The despair and self-disgust that comes with a food or alcohol hangover or that follow a period of acting out sexually might be enough for a nonaddicted person to say, "Boy, I really messed up; I'll never do that again!" and stick to that decision. The memory serves as sufficient incentive to avoid the behavior. But for the addict, the reemergence of the pain only triggers the urge to act out all over again. Their activity becomes a vicious cycle; they do what they do as if they have no choice.

The urge to act out can be broken into two phases: preoccupation and ritualization. Both phases are significant for codependents and particularly for church codependents.

Preoccupation, for a codependent, is obsessive thinking about the significant other: what is worrying him, what she might like, what the codependent might do to make this other person's life better (and make the codependent loved and accepted), or what the codependent might do to make the other change.

For church codependents, negative emotions trigger preoccupation over ways to be helpful (translate: ways to be needed), to keep everyone happy and doing what we want, or with ways to make the family or the other person look good or change. Every conversation gets around to "What can we do to fix this?" "I can't just let the program die," or "Somebody has to get Father to change." Time is spent in obsessive concern over ways to save single-handedly the church. That is the preoccupation phase.

Ritual is sacred to addicts. Each step of their well-practiced rite serves to lift them out of the disappointing world of reality and into the anesthetized state where they are comforted, sure of themselves, and in control.

Ritual is also an important part of our Christian expression. How can we know the difference between healthy ritual and the ritual that is part of an addictive cycle? The goals of healthy ritual are to state a belief, making it more conscious, and to act out that belief in some simple way, so that we gradually change our behavior in and out of church to reflect more closely our beliefs. To the extent that our ritual actions make us more conscious of our relationship with God and others in our day-to-day life and help us to live out our faith in the real world, we are engaging in healthy ritual, what some denominations call sacrament.

If our desire is to escape from reality into a warm haze where we can avoid what we do not want to face and where we can feel reassured that we are safe but helpless children, we may be using religious ritual the same way some use alcohol or drugs, for mood-altering, anesthetizing, making the world go away.

For instance, some Christians break bread together to celebrate our covenant with each other and with God, to reenact Jesus' Passover meal, and to remember his presence with us. Healthy participation in that ritual should gradually make us more conscious of our commitment to be covenant family and should gradually change our behavior in and out of church, so that our daily actions better reflect that commitment. On the other hand, the ritual can be used as a warm place for escape, anesthetizing the rest of our life rather than transforming it.

Addictive ritual extends beyond formal ceremonies; it includes any regular pattern of actions that is pursued because it leads up to or creates an elevated mood. We can keep ourselves in a warm haze of unreality by dressing in religious garb, praying in a rhythmic chant, clinging to the notion that we are the last bastion of goodness in a world being taken over by the devil, going through cycles of programs that divert attention from life, or by using titles (calling someone "Father" implies I am a child, safe and without responsibility). We can keep statistics on how many of "us" there are, how many stations carry our broadcasts, how much money we have collected toward our next building, how many people we have serviced on a given Sunday, how many listened to the preacher or the pope. All these diversions and many more keep us busy and isolated in our own little world. They divert our energies and creativity from the mission of living Jesus' down-to-earth gospel in the real world.

The next part of the cycle is compulsive behavior. A codependent wife will move from preoccupation and ritualization to compulsive action, will "perform" all she planned and more, trying to make her husband happy or win him over to show her affection. If the spouse is not receptive or rejects the elaborate meal or the special time together or the gift of the codependent herself, she will keep going after him, keep giving herself away, keep pleading or crying for acceptance even in the face of cold rejection or abuse. That is the nature of compulsive/addictive activity: the addict continues as if life depended on it, as if she has no choice.

Church codependents donate funds without limit and without question, even when the amount of the donation jeopardizes their own economic survival, even when their "man of God" has been exposed as a fraud. Older people and young adults have been conned into signing over all the savings they have to some very "caring" religious leader. And some would give it all again, convinced that there was no wrongdoing, but that the "powers of evil" set up the evidence to stop this "holy" man.

Church codependents pour tremendous energy into rescuing or protecting their institution, even when the institutional powers reject them and their efforts. When the Vatican held a world synod on the "laity" (their word, not mine) a couple of years ago, a meeting to which no laity were invited, an organization of American lay Catholics held their own meeting in Rome so that their input would be available. Obviously, the availability of their input was never the issue: the Vatican wanted only clerical opinions in the discussion. The organization invested many dollars and hours to produce the meeting, only to be surprised and disappointed when the pope failed to make use of their ideas.

People who are trying to change the institution by changing the hierarchy are subject to periods of despair, periods in which they consider cutting all ties to any kind of faith community. Carnes says that the despair phase "combines the sense of failure at not having lived up to resolutions to stop, with hopelessness about ever being able to stop" (Carnes, *Out of the Shadows*, 12). It includes self-pity, self-hatred, shame, and possibly suicidal feelings. For the codependent, despair involves feelings of utter worthlessness at having failed to make the whole parish or the whole pastoral staff happy and involved, despair that the relationship is drifting apart in spite of every effort to sustain it. But, and this is the sign of addiction, instead of despair leading to a healthier alternative, the despair is the pain that leads to more preoccupation, and the cycle begins again. Often those down periods are followed by spurts of new energy, bigger ideas, and more church work, trying one more time to make *them* change.

Unmanageability — The Addiction Takes Over

Like any addiction, we can begin pursuing any of our mood-altering activities occasionally, by choice, and then progress to the point where we feel we must have them at any cost or sacrifice and we will not tolerate anyone who stands in the way of our being satisfied. The four-phase cycle repeats itself until it takes over our lives. In the words of Alcoholics Anonymous, our lives become unmanageable.

Codependents tend to overfunction to the point of self-destruction. The more one tries to carry the responsibilities both of one's own life and the life of the church institution, the more fatigue and stress take their toll on health. The desperate drive to control a doomed relationship exhausts all the energy and attention that are needed in other areas of life, so those other commitments and responsibilities begin to fall apart.

As the addiction takes over, fatigue and the resulting failure in other important areas of life cause one to be less "on top of things"; one feels less able to function on any level. As performance levels decline, the negative experiences reinforce the already destructive set of core beliefs. One becomes more convinced that: "I am an unworthy person; I am fortunate to have this church (or spiritual advisor or position); surely no one else would want me now. Even the church would not want me if they knew what a mess I'm in. The only way to save myself is to hang onto this relationship, even if everything else is lost."

Ironically, this clinging attitude allows the "significant other" or those representing the institution to be even more distant, more abusive: the codependent will put up with anything to hold onto the relationship. The more controlling or abusive our target person or institution becomes toward us, and the more we take it, the more we tend to see ourselves as worthless. We conclude that, since we are treated this way by "Holy Mother Church," no one else would like us either: "If I cannot lead Bible study for the institutional church, there is no other place in the world where I can use that gift."

The belief that the institutional church has the power to grant one personal value results in a sense of valuelessness when that approval is withheld. That leads to a sense of powerlessness in normal activities, even in areas of one's own professional competence, because the church is not supportive. Objective, functional failure follows the belief that one is no good, that one cannot perform. For the codependent, the introduction of any part of this thought process inevitably feeds into the addictive cycle. Without a recovery program to change the thinking process, codependents are without choice in their pursuit of relationships and are, therefore, addicted.

Since all codependents, including those in church, tend to gravitate toward persons who may be publicly charming but privately cold, distant, and not really there for them, they are constantly looking for help from people who cannot give it. Home and church compound the problem. How many women and men escape from their empty codependent relationships at home into addictive relationships with the leaders, meetings, and rituals of organized religion, in an attempt to anesthetize the pain, only to find themselves used and abused again? From this dismal set of experiences, one can easily see why the codependent would project that no one in the world is dependable. The only thing left, the one thing codependents can depend on, is their own willingness to give up their centers and the consequent illusion of togetherness they experience when they do that.

There are codependent women who feel more desire for men who abuse them than for those who care for them (see Robin Norwood, *Women Who Love Too Much*). Similarly in church, the rush of excitement that comes from trying to be all things to all people, trying to change the unchangeable, or trying to do enough to bring about the desired results in others can be so stimulating and emotionally all-consuming that it feels like a "total relationship." The intensity of the desire, self-sacrifice, and pain can have a more powerful attraction than the serenity of an easier, or even satisfying, church experience.

A codependent relationship to church may provide nothing that we might expect from simple, authentic church, none of the nutritional requirements that church is supposed to provide. Codependent busy-ness and worry are to true Christian community and ministry as junk food is to a balanced diet of nutritious food. Unhealthy as it is, it still tempts some to take handful after handful; and though it gives little in the way of real nourishment, it does fill up the feeling of emptiness, the hole in one's center. Codependent religious activity can become such a habit that it can make a healthy church, a small community with true community support and spiritual nourishment, seem boring by comparison.

Double Lives, Lies, and Multiple Addictions

When self-esteem rests on another person or system, particularly an unreliable one, the world appears chaotic, even hostile. Suspicion and paranoia are common codependent traits and are clearly in evidence in certain closed and rigid church systems. The world is seen as a hostile environment; only we in the fold are safe.

Within some codependent church systems, there is a constant blaming of others for "causing" so much extra work: "If only *they* (the pastors, the bishops, the central assembly, the members) would change, my life would be better." In actuality, any evidence of real systemic change in their parent church — growth, mutuality, recovery — would probably send the codependent looking for another sick institution, another congregation that would welcome their nonproductive busyness.

Physical symptoms manifest the stress of the codependent relationship. Our bodies signal "S.O.S." even when our conscious minds have refused to acknowledge there is a problem. Symptoms include gastrointestinal problems, headaches, back, shoulder, or neck pain, skin rashes, insomnia, food allergies, respiratory difficulties, heart irregularities, and hypertension. Even cancer has been tied to the kind of chronic stress that is typical of codependence. Like the physical anguish that accompanies withdrawal from any addiction, these physical symptoms commonly increase if the codependent relationship is lost or threatened.

Another negative consequence of codependence is depression, anger turned inward. We sense the situation is hopeless, yet our identity is tied to working to fix it. We hate ourselves for being fools, hate the others for being abusive, and yet cannot bring ourselves to let go. The cycle is self-destructive.

"One of the worst consequences of addiction is the addicts' isolation. The intensity of the double life relates directly to the distance of the addicts from their friends and family. That is, the more intensely involved in compulsive (addictive) life the addicts become, the more alienated they become from their parents, spouses, and children. Without those human connections, the addicts paradoxically lose touch with their own selves. The unmanageability of the addiction has run its course when there is no longer a double life" — because the addiction has taken over the addict's whole life (Carnes, *Out Of the Shadows*, 13, 14).

As the addicts sink further into their addiction, they pull away from anyone who can see what is happening, anyone who expects them to be intimate and honest, any true friends. They gravitate toward the equivalent of "drinking buddies," people who will support them in their denial. Chapter 5 discussed double lives among some church workers: living the illusion of celibacy or marriage while carrying on multiple affairs or one long-term relationship in secret.

Maintaining the denial becomes ever more difficult as the negative consequences of the addiction become more obvious, and so the lies become more frequent. As described in chapter 8, addicts move from denial into delusion, and actually come to believe their own lies. Lies are used in church as a big, dark tarpaulin, to cover the vulnerable areas of power, money, and sex.

The further from reality that addicts go, the more difficult it is to face themselves or the real world. It is not uncommon for addicts to seek relief from their pain and self-disgust in another addiction. Since addictions are all motivated by the same set of core beliefs, it is possible and even likely that that self-destructive set of beliefs is generating more than one addiction. These other addictions are concurrent illnesses that must also be treated for the addict to recover. If they are not addressed, the cessation of one kind of compulsive activity will only shift the compulsion to another. Church codependents can also be addicted to nicotine, sedatives, grandiosity, gossip, books, bingo, workshops, food, alcohol, sex, or power.

The Church's Two Addictions

Organized religion, in this time and culture, is plagued by two related addictions: security and power. We start by depending on institutional religion for security. Some will do or believe or give anything to maintain that security. Others go a step farther, see more security in positions of power, and develop a drive for power.

The two compulsions complement each other. Those who want only security are looking for a child's position in the family system. They need someone else to hold the power. "If the pope does not know all the answers, then who does? Somebody must!" They want Pastor or Father to know more than they do, to take responsibility for their spirituality, to take care of them.

Those who crave security-through-power need someone else to acknowledge their power, someone to depend on them and help them feel stronger or higher than the rest. Their vested interest is not in helping their "flock" to grow to healthy autonomy and interdependence, but in keeping them dependent and deferential.

Years ago, in the early days of word processors, there were military officers on the Pentagon staff who resisted the acquisition of programmable typewriters because they would make office work too efficient. Their rank depended on their having many staff persons under them. Better use of personnel would mean less power, and was therefore undesirable.

Today virtually no one has a domestic staff to wait on table during meals: what statement are we making about power in the Christian community by retaining the use of altar servers to wait on Pastor or Father at the church table? It certainly was not Jesus' style.

It is a sign of dysfunction that codependents give away their own power over their lives and choices to someone else; it is also a sign of dysfunction that someone would want or accept that kind of power over someone else's life. "Those who do usually possess a narcissistic need to be considered special. Chemical dependents in the active phase of their disease, and persons with personality or impulse disorders, have this need" (Timmen Cermak, *Diagnosing and Treating Co-dependence*, 21). Only those in the active stages of addiction or those with narcissistic tendencies would have such a grandiose sense of their own power that they would be willing to accept that kind of responsibility for others' lives. Those who think it to their benefit to keep codependents codependent are themselves addicted to the feeling of power and the psychological high that comes with the power.

The security-seekers and the power-seekers complement each other and have a vested interest in keeping one another in those roles. Both groups maintain and operate out of a logic that makes no sense outside their own closed system. Both groups do unreasonable things as if they had no choice. Both groups tolerate unreasonable things as if they had no choice. Both groups insist that the status quo, this unhealthy balance, be maintained as if they had no choice. This is the pattern of an addictive family system: we need to keep each other sick to insulate our own sickness from the truth.

Jesus was nailed to the cross because he was *not* codependent; authentic following of Jesus requires women and men with the same kind of courageous autonomy, willing to take the risks and take the consequences. Much of organized religion today requires instead security-addicted codependents and power-addicted codependents who would rather hand over their centers than use them, who would rather feign death than face it.

Jesus and the Established Church

It is helpful, occasionally, to read the gospel substituting "church" for "temple" or "synagogue" so that we can hear more clearly how the gospel speaks to us. We Christians tend to hear Jesus' words addressed to his religious tradition; we do not realize clearly enough that his words were directed to all advocates of religion for its own sake, that he spoke to a tension in every faith group before and since, including our own.

Jesus was a good and faithful Jew. He never said that what his people were about was bad or obsolete. He and his students gathered regularly for Sabbath suppers, to remember God's care and give thanks for it, to remember their covenant responsibilities to God and to each other, and to celebrate community. He prayed and read the Scriptures. He went to church. But he took issue with enough sacred traditions to incur the wrath of his own religious leaders: he had dinner at the houses of non-believers; he disregarded some "unquestionable" customs; he said that making peace with others came before ritual; he said service to the real needs of real people was more important than church duties; he said love was the most important part of the law; he said that the church *building* was not the greatest sign of God's presence.

Jesus was open to change, daring in his criticism of the established religion, which was his own religion, and heroic in practicing what he preached.

It does not make sense for us — in Jesus' name — to praise ourselves for having such pure vision when that vision is limited to what we want to see, to take pride in our fidelity when we are faithful to archaic, man-made traditions. It is not a sign of fidelity to Jesus to glory in the pain of our self-inflicted wounds. What we have been doing in the name of fidelity may have been acts of cowardice, compulsion, and addiction.

Jesus lived and preached a message of simplicity and service: God first, people first, religion as expression and support. His voice reached the alienated and touched the sick and the poor. He had choices, times when he knew that friends and family would not understand why he spoke out, times when he knew he was digging his own grave. Some of us have known times like that. He could have gone along with the program and kept his thoughts to himself, but he did not. He could have kept a low profile and avoided trouble, but he did not.

It was for standing up to the religious authorities in his own church that Jesus was delivered over to be tortured and executed. Like many religious bodies before and since, they found a political way of dispatching a "troublemaker." It was underhanded and over-reactive, but it did protect the church. It was masterminded by a few and carried out with the easy assistance of a mindless crowd, but it did protect the church.

Everyone cut out their centers and handed them over to the religious leaders; and those few who held all the centers, those few who were still making decisions said, "Crucify him!" And the many, who thought what they were told to think and felt what they were told to feel and did what they were told to do, echoed, "Crucify him!" And the one who still had his own center, who claimed his own freedom and left others the freedom to keep their centers, went to his death alone.

In his center, in the deepest part of himself, Jesus had room to know and listen to God. In that center, he chose not to pass by but to stop and help the hurting, whatever their affiliation. In his center, he held his own priorities, priorities different from those of the group "in charge." In his center, he saw the risks and repeatedly chose to take those risks. When he was given a last choice, an ultimatum, he chose to die rather than to hand over his center and become one more automaton reciting churchspeak. When he said, "Into your hands I commend my spirit," that spirit was still his and was still whole.

Crucify Us — Dead Is Easier!

When Jesus shared his Spirit with his followers, it was an invitation for communion between his Spirit and our own, between his center and our own. Unfortunately, many Christian centers are no longer at home.

Jesus modeled a way of life that required no credentials — proof that one does not need a Ph.D. to be silenced — but did call for courage and initiative. He invited us to do what he did, to move about in wholeness and freedom, to use all our God-given creative energy to break down walls and build up the family of God.

I think all of us must have felt that call, that exhilaration of being able to act and ready to start, at least once. Many of us have looked, taken a step, and moved back into the security of our codependence, where we can remain forever docile children, responsible only for cleaning our rooms, while we let "Papa" or "Holy Mother" take care of all the big decisions.

The Day of the Lord, the family of God, the way Jesus preached it and lived it, should have unleashed tremendous energy, tremendous creativity, tremendous power for good. And the power is in us, in all of us, in all of creation. But instead of embracing the power, we cower in fear. We are afraid of the power in our own centers, and so we cut them out and hand them over.

We lie down on the cross of our own choosing and ask for the nails of blind obedience, bigotry, triumphalism, sexism, nationalism, homophobia, arrogance, blissful ignorance. It is easier to be nailed down and secure than to take the risks of being rejected by family or friends or church leaders. It is easier to be nailed down and wait for future deliverance than to take the risks to address the problems of today. It is easier to be nailed down and secure than to take the risks of responding to the needs of the earth that make us shudder, needs of humankind that overwhelm us. No matter that addiction is a pathology of church, that codependence destroys life. After all, as long as we are nailed down, we will be like Jesus: Jesus suffered too.

11

Intervention and the End of Enabling

In everyone's life, somewhere between the age of eighteen and twenty-eight, or for some as late as thirty-eight or forty-eight, there comes a time when one knows what one must do, does it, and does not ask permission.

I know adults in their thirties and forties who have made a conscious choice to eat light and exercise regularly, not just for appearance, but for a better quality of life and health. It pains them that their parents, through all their adult years, have been eating big, heavy meals, smoking, and spending their free time sitting in front of the television. It pains them to see their parents reaping the health problems they have sown. But they, the adult children, recognize that they themselves will be the ones to live with the consequences of their own choices long after their parents have gone, and so they have given themselves permission to choose another lifestyle.

There comes a time when one can face one's parents and say, "I love you very much, and I know that you may not understand why I am doing this, but I have given this matter much thought and I know that this is what I must do. I love you very much, but this is my choice." We have probably said it, in word or in action, to our parents. Now we must say that to our parent churches.

We Are Not Dependent Children

We are not dependent children of our parent churches. All parties are adults; we all have to make and live with our own decisions. There are other adults who make up that parent church, other persons to whom it seems the safer, more comfortable course to continue doing what they have done for as long as they can remember, ending their days with a rich, heavy meal and a cigar, spending a few hours in an easy chair watching an old drama in which "mindless" women and "powerful" men play out their predictable roles. We cannot make them change, but we do not have to emulate them.

This means that if we are ready for a community that does not hold the only franchise on God, but offers support for simple living and open-handed generosity, a community that communicates openly and honestly, a community which is not stratified but in which all are co-responsible, both expected and welcomed to use their gifts regardless of gender, race, age, or sexual orientation, a community in which we celebrate God's presence and direction in everyday life, then we are responsible to pursue development of that kind of community, whether other members of our parent church are ready to change or not. We cannot change other persons or systems, but we can change ourselves.

The choice not to repeat the choices of our parents is the first hurdle; the second is more difficult yet: letting go of the urge to force our parents to change.

Healthy relationships with older parents and with adult sons and daughters should be characterized by a respectful detachment. We can advise them, we can celebrate or grieve with them over the consequences of their decisions, but when it comes to making the decisions, we need to let go. True, we are going to be touched by those decisions in some ways, but neither our adult sons and daughters nor our older parents are our dependent children. Neither the clergy nor the incoming members of our churches are our dependent children. All are adults; none has to be protected; we all have to make and live with our own decisions.

Some recovering Christians, though, feel tremendous anguish at their parent churches' self-destructive choices. They desire so strongly to be able to reach those addicted to power, to have them listen and change, but those efforts perpetuate the system. There is only one known process for reaching addicts, and it carries no guarantees.

Intervention

There is a saying in addiction circles that one has to "hit bottom" before one seeks recovery, that one has to lose enough that the pain finally breaks through the denial. Extending that image, we say it is possible to "raise the bottom," to bring about that crisis point sooner. This is done by a process called intervention.

The process begins with the gathering of persons who are close to the troubled individual: family, close friends, and, if possible, the employer. The employer is asked both because of the monetary leverage that that person has, and, since in-patient treatment requires twenty-one days away from work, because the employer's understanding and cooperation will be needed. Keep in mind here that, in the case of church, it is the members who are the "employers," in the sense that we ultimately pay the salaries and expenses of leaders and institutions.

During the preparation period before the intervention, the group of concerned individuals meets with a trained intervention counsellor to learn about addiction: that they did not cause and cannot cure it, but that their own words and actions have been enabling the dysfunction by cooperating in the addict's denial. They consider that the only healthy option they have is to stop enabling. They commit themselves to confronting the addict and promise each other that they will no longer do anything to enable.

The intervention itself is a meeting in which these people confront the addict. The same counsellor who led the preparation will facilitate the confrontation. Each reads from a prewritten letter detailing first-hand experiences of the person's "acting out," or doing their addiction. They also tell of the physical and emotional repercussions they have experienced as a result of those actions. Each participant expresses love and care for the addict, and the desire to see the addict recover. And finally, the addict is told which treatment program the family has selected (a room will have already been reserved, a suitcase packed, and all necessary arrangements made with the person's employer). He or she is asked to come along *right now* to that facility.

If the addict refuses, there are strong consequences; sometimes the addict's job is on the line. In any case, the family members and friends make it very clear, to the addict and to each other, that they all know that this is an addiction and that they will not enable the dysfunction in any way, any longer.

Whatever the addict decides, and this is most important for our purposes here, those who participate in the intervention or prepare for an intervention are themselves radically changed. Once they have acknowledged openly the extent of the damage the addiction has done to them, it is very difficult to crawl back into a state of denial. Once they have pledged publicly to refrain from any kind of enabling, they have both group pressure and group support to follow through with that commitment. So whether the addict decides to accept treatment or not, things will not be the same at home or at work, or at church.

It might be helpful for us to do an intervention, but without trying to get any institutional church to change. To assemble enough people to create the impact of an intervention would require gathering a substantial portion of the membership of that church. Even if that could be accomplished, it would not be enough to convince some church leaders to change. Part of the problem of religious addiction is that God is seen to be ratifying the compulsive behavior, so the whole world could be assembled on the other side and the addicts still would not "abandon God" by altering their pattern of behavior.

The statements that follow were written as letters of intervention. In a sense, this entire book is an intervention. But the goal is not to change the institutional church. To do an intervention with the hope of changing the church would be just one more act of codependence. But sharing in a process of intervention can be a milestone for codependent Christians, even if the institutions do not listen at all. Those who participate share their experiences, label the problem, and make a commitment, to themselves and to one another, that they will no longer enable dysfunction. Intervention can be an occasion for church members to begin to change ourselves, to begin our own recovery from codependence together.

The Letters

Church member to bishop:

Just last week you announced that all the white parishes would remain open, but that most of the parishes in black and Hispanic neighborhoods would have to close. The white, middle-class parishes give you more money. You announced these closings without any chance for people to feed back or react or ask questions. You just read a letter at the end of Mass and sent us all out. Now my brothers and sisters with brown and black skin will have no home, but you would not let us respond.

A lot of people felt angry, but they didn't think they could talk to you. They didn't think you would listen. They didn't think it would help. Everyone was afraid you would be angry if we disturbed you.

Parish leader to pastor:

Before you came, we had developed a parish where Hispanics could appreciate their history, culture, and religiosity and develop their own leadership, not in competition but to fulfill the dream that all people should be co-responsible. What we have is not evil, but it is different. It is our own.

You look at our past as boring and see our accomplishments as nothing, because according to your way of seeing things, we are not organized and do not follow the books. We have a vision as a people, and gradually we want that peopleness to create its own leadership and process of growth according to the cultural values of our people.

You used your role to humble and create division within the community. You found all sorts of things to criticize about us; you threw out our mission statements and constitution as though everything we did God was never part of. We are no longer *mudos* [mute] and *ignorantes*. We have learned to talk and communicate our God life, because we have lived it and felt the presence of God among us as well as any other parish. WE know that this parish is not the work of one person or movement. We feel we have been used as second-rate Christians.

Church organization member to pastor:

You were going to attend one of our meetings and had invited us all to lunch with you afterward. You spent the first half of the meeting in the next room with your back to us. Then you neglected to inform the cook that our guests were expecting to be fed. I could kick myself now for the enabling behavior on my part — quietly giving that information to the cook.

A former parish volunteer to others involved in parish activities:

I wish I had known about codependency before becoming a lay minister in my parish. I would have bailed out much sooner.

My parish is very conservative; changes are superficial and clergy maintain all the power and control. With lots of energy, experience, and enthusiasm, I tried to soften the barriers so that the needs of people would be met. This was unrealistic; open communication, flexibility, mutual support, and being involved in the decision making was not part of the process. Being a lay minister meant serving as a mirror for clergy, giving up more and more of my initiative and imagination until not much of the real me was left to give. As a facilitator, I was really a girl Friday, a hospitality person, and a prop. Unfortunately, it took a sudden blow to see this clearly.

One of the priests took offense at a question I asked in one of his classes for candidates, a question concerning the lack of a parish council. I guess this was a violation of the party line. He portrayed me as a disruptive person to the three other priests involved and, without benefit of a hearing, I was relieved of my ministry. When I questioned this "kangaroo court" method, the "brotherhood of priests" was the reason given. My request to speak directly to the brotherhood was refused.

From a pastor:

I was serving as part-time pastor of a tiny Baptist church in New England. One night I came home very disturbed after a long meeting with the church governing boards. We had been discussing the "needs of our church" and "our response." At each turn, "our response" was for me to meet the need. By the end of the evening I was feeling overwhelmed and angry.

I knew I was a good pastor, skilled at many tasks pastoral ministry includes, yet I couldn't respond single-handedly to all the "church's needs."

During the meeting I asked the boards to prioritize the tasks I had been given so that we could agree on which would get attention and which not. It felt awkward setting limits instead of fulfilling expectations, telling the boards I would not and could not be the savior of our church.

That night, at home, I wrote these verses:

> Ah, Lord, your church;
> She is like a very beautiful,
> Very fickle woman.

If I bring her diamonds,
It is pearls she craves.
Bring her pearls,
She wants rubies.

(It goes on a few more stanzas.)

The next day I decided to retain my sense of integrity in all I did with this or any congregation. My journey toward recovery had begun.

Priest to other priests and church workers:

The only way to work in this sick system and stay sane is to be working a Twelve Step program. The healthy ones are doing that. But it is hard to go into recovery for alcoholism, for codependence, or as an adult child of an alcoholic and still work for the institution. The perspective from recovery is so different from that of those still in denial. It is never okay with non-recovering family members that you begin recovery. Those trying to become healthy are regarded as "the problem."

Parish education administrator to junior pastor:

You have a serious problem dealing with women and label any female who disagrees with you as an "angry woman." When this happens to me, I find myself living up to your label because it alone is enough to make me seethe inside.

You disrupted a committee meeting by arguing with decisions made at a previous meeting, one to which you were invited but had failed to attend; you wanted to rearrange our calendar, tried to control us, and finally resorted to personal attacks against me.

At this point, I am trying to resist the move toward chronic cynicism. It isn't easy. After many years of working for the parish and having had the opportunity to observe more closely the workings of the parish, I feel lucky to keep any sense of hope at all.

I heard a pastor at a conference say that we are in an addictive system, struggling to cope with authority figures who are helpless addicts. He said we need to develop our inner liberation, that we have to be free enough to love and to accept the addicts while not enabling them any more and not allowing them to manipulate us. He said that until we have bottomed out we cannot be free enough to confront or to engage in respectful disagreement. I think I am on the verge of bottoming out.

Parish member to pastor:

I am writing to say that I love you; because of that, I will no longer support you or cover up for you. I know that you are good inside, but because you are drunk with power, you have been hurting me and my family.

You wanted to build a new church building at Saint Unknown parish. To justify the building to the parishioners and to the bishop, you started creating inflated reports about the number of parishioners. Then you invented phoney demographic data. You just kept on building the lie and piling lie upon lie to get the building. I know because I checked with both the census bureau and with the diocesan planning office to get the true numbers.

When I pointed this out to you, you attacked me verbally and psychologically, dismantled the parish committee I was running, defamed me to other parishioners, and finally took my name off the parish roles. I tried other channels, but the diocesan newspaper rebuffed me, and the chancery office replied that it "fully supported" what the pastor was doing.

My spouse and I were devastated by your attacks. I wanted you to get better, but I could never get through. You would never listen. You would only react by grabbing one more fix of power and authority and use it to silence me or embarrass me or hurt me.

I now realize that I am powerless to do anything to force you to change; only you can change you. I can only change myself and my own actions, and I *have* changed my own actions.

Change-back Tactics: What If the Worst Happened?

What would happen if we stopped reacting and enabling? In a dysfunctional family, when one member tries to take steps toward recovery, other members will often try to sabotage that effort with threats or other abusive tactics designed to bring the recovering person back into line, back into that person's role in the dysfunction. Women and men who join Twelve Step programs to change their own codependent behavior and cope with their spouses' addictions often find that their spouses will act out (e.g., get drunk) every time they go to a meeting, or will fail to come home in time to care for the children or will be home but neglect the children during the meeting. The addicts rule by fear and intimidation. They are delivering a message: change back!

As long as everyone plays by the rules of dysfunction, those kinds of intimidation always work: fear forces conformity to the old, sick rules of the game. Those who are serious about recovery, however, cannot afford to let those tactics prevail.

The way out of the fear is to face the worst. Ask, "What is the worst that can happen?" and figure out what you would do if it did. Facing our fears takes the terror out of them. We would not choose to have those threats carried out, but since we are powerless over other people, we have no control over that. We would not choose to have to deal with those problems, but once we have chosen to get well, we must face the fears that keep us codependent. We would not choose to have to make those choices on our own, but we come to learn that we are stronger than we thought, and that, with God and the recovering friends we meet in program, we are never alone.

What would happen if the people living in those dioceses where churches and schools have been closed with no responsible input from the parishioners would simply cease contributing until there is local ownership and complete mutual accountability? What if they opted for no more talk, no more protests, just a responsible change in their own behavior?

Economic boycott would bring about the worst kinds of threats — closings, firings, discontinuation of services — and some of them would be carried out. Those involved would have to keep their focus and keep their resolve through it all, until they reached the goal of local ownership and accountability, modified by some ideal of simplicity and sharing.

What would happen if, instead of putting money into the basket, the parishioners elected a committee of neighbors to open a new bank account for the payment of utilities? At worst, the people would have to find another place to gather; many are facing that already because the decision is being made for them. The clergy have married and now teach or do social work; the buildings are being sold. Those who do make provisions would at least have a space to gather that could not be taken from them.

What would happen if the powers-that-be discovered that small groups were meeting in homes and other unholy places, without clergy,

for Bible study or support or prayer or even communion? In some denominations, if the local bishop or leader is very controlling or looking
over his shoulder for approval, there might be a threat or an announcement of excommunication: "Fie! Get thee hence!" Then where do you
suppose those communities would be — inside or outside the circle of
church? It depends on who is drawing the circle, does it not? It depends
on what criteria are used for drawing the circle over here instead of over
there, for making the radius very small instead of very big. A poem I
read years ago keeps coming back to me:

> He drew a circle that shut me out —
> Heretic, rebel, a thing to flout.
> But Love and I had the wit to win:
> We drew a circle that took him in.

Edwin Markham, "Outwitted"

The early Christians were on the outside of the circle as it was drawn
by their own denomination. But they looked to the gospel message as
their focus, kept that center in the center, and tried to live within the
circle that it created, by fidelity to that message.

Those who draw their circle to cut us out may later come to see
things differently. They may begin recovery themselves and come to
understand what we were trying to do. Then again, they may not ever
change. We can neither control nor predict that: we are powerless over
the behavior of others. But we are responsible for our own.

We can love and respect our parent churches as persons who have
given us much over the years and to whom we are grateful. At the same
time, we recognize that they are persons with whom we respectfully disagree. We have the right and the responsibility to make the best choices
we can, as we understand things, and acknowledge that they have the
right to do the same. That those choices are different does not make
either party bad; it is just the way things are.

Part IV

Recovery

12

From the Inside Out

Any addiction affects our attitudes and behaviors in many ways not immediately identifiable with the "drug." We may talk or act irrationally even when not "under the influence"; we may lie, blame, control, manipulate. We may keep ourselves behind an impenetrable wall or in a state of willed confusion to hide from the world, from our colleagues and families, from ourselves, and from the truth.

In the case of any addiction, there is no recovery without abstinence. Our addiction masks the real problem, alters our mood, reinforces our denial and isolation. There is no way to get at the painful feelings that the addiction is anesthetizing, no way to reach the core beliefs and correct them, as long as the preoccupation and mood-altering effect of the addiction keeps them all beyond our reach.

Some trying to recover from addiction to drugs or alcohol enter resident treatment programs to ensure a month of abstinence; after that they will be better able to say no on their own. Recovery from food addiction depends on abstinence from those foods and eating patterns that one has misused, so that one can confront the long buried feelings and beliefs that kept the addiction going. Sex addicts are advised to abstain completely from any sexual activity while they get in touch with and work through all the insecurities, low self-esteem, and long-hidden memories that compel them to act out sexually.

For a codependent, abstinence means fasting from emotional involvement — we call that "detachment" — and fasting from reactive behavior.

Detachment

Detachment operates like the clutch of a car, disengaging the gears from each other so that one can change gears without damaging them. Detachment disengages my thoughts and actions from the abusive or irrational behavior I am experiencing, so that the other person's craziness does not "turn my wheels."

Detachment is the refusal to "get hooked" by the insanity around us. When codependents do "get hooked," we slide right into the preoccupation phase of our addiction: we begin to be obsessed with the words, moods, and behaviors of the other person or group. We spend hours going over what that person or group might like and how pleased they would be if we would take care of this matter for them, or what they might be thinking and how we might be able to change them. The preoccupation phase heightens the mood and readies mind and body for moving into addictive behavior. Detachment is staying out of that preoccupation.

A codependent living in a repressive system or with an active addict must learn to detach, to tune out, when the person or group "talks crazy," whether the words are abusive, sweet, cunning, or manipulative. Sometimes the only way to tune out is to get out, to leave the room or the house, to leave Sunday worship or the committee meeting, for as long as it takes to let go of it all emotionally, to get recentered, to reclaim what AA people call serenity. Community worship and other activities should help us live faithfully; we should not have to struggle to live faithfully *in spite of* them.

Detachment means telling oneself "I do have a choice: I do not have to let this person abuse or manipulate me. I will not allow this person to abuse or con me. For now, I will leave the situation. Later, when I am calm, free, and able to think more clearly, I will decide how to handle this."

Eventually, one can learn to detach while still in the presence of crazy talk and behavior. But most of the time, I'm afraid, it is too easy to fool oneself into thinking it does not matter, when in fact all the abusive or cunning words are making an impression. We see ourselves degraded or helpless once again. It is better not to reinforce that image, not to expose ourselves to that kind of bullying. We need to begin to identify certain verbal deliveries as abuse or a con immediately and to step out of the situation lest we give in to the urge to be obsessed with it or to react to it.

Some recovering Christians resign from church committee work until they are confident that they will not give up their centers. Some find they need to abstain from any attendance at or involvement in any institutional church functions for a year or more until they have made a solid start to their recovery and can recognize dysfunction rather than be pulled back into it.

One couple involved in a small community church in St. Louis found it easy to get out of the institutional church, but much more difficult to get the institutional church out of them. They said they have made a conscious decision to "fast from institutional religion" for as long as it takes to get those methods of thinking and acting out of their systems.

Some career church personnel who work in the system are discovering that their more recognizable addictions — alcohol, work, food, sex — are masking an addiction to church. Those in that situation will have to work out a clear definition of what will constitute abstinence for them — perhaps refraining from any institutional involvement, at least for a time — in order to begin recovery. For them, small community involvement will have to be their only church experience.

No More Reacting

Reaction to others is the codependent's own addictive behavior. Once we have become obsessed to a point of sufficient inner tension, we feel the compulsion to act, or, in this case, to react to the dynamics that were initiated by the focal person or group. We operate out of an addictive drive to react in unhealthy ways; we tell ourselves, "Somebody's got to do it," or "It might work *this* time." Typical of all addictions, the more painful the situation becomes, the more futile it all seems, the more we react. The more disgusted we are with ourselves for having interfered unwisely, or for having been used, the more we do.

It is very difficult for a codependent to let go, to not react. For as long as some of us can remember, we have always hung on, our minds spinning wildly in search of a response, and then engaged the other(s) with a barrage of questions, defenses, arguments, and explanations, all attempts to win over the other side, as if this was a logical conversation in the first place. Others of us, for as long as we can remember, have always been ready to agree with, to placate, to smooth over, or to try to please this person or group we think we need more than life. These two approaches appear very different, but they are not.

Whether we are attempting to reach the others aggressively in order to win them over or trying to calm and please them, we are reacting. Someone pushes our buttons and we jump into action; someone starts playing the music, and we automatically begin to dance.

We operate from two false assumptions: that if we do not do our usual reacting, we will lose the relationship, and that if we lose the relationship, we will perish. But our reactive behavior perpetuates the very hurtful pattern we abhor and contributes to the deterioration of the relationship; and remaining in that sick system is more harmful to us than leaving.

The other person or system can count on us to do what we do — this is not a solo dance — and when we behave predictably, everyone remains comfortable, for this is what the whole system has come to consider as normal. No one needs to think or to reconsider or to change. We have all silently agreed to continue dancing in the same way we have been practicing for years. We dance until we are completely exhausted, until there is no life left in us.

The focal person receives just what he or she expected — familiar feedback — which actually provides some relief for his or her own inner stress. The more emotional the reaction is, the more relief it probably provides. Then the symptom-bearer mellows out, the codependent breathes a sigh of relief, and the problem appears to be over. Things go back to "normal" for a time, and then, "unexpectedly," it all begins again. The symptom may have been alleviated, but the chronic condition persists.

In Chicago, the archbishop announced the closing of twenty-two parish churches; a year or so earlier the archbishop in Detroit had announced that forty-seven churches there would close. None of the people who belonged to those parishes, whose families had built both the communities and the buildings, was involved in those decisions. There was no local ownership, no involvement of the people in balancing expenses against income, no knowledge of the bigger diocesan financial picture, no community struggle with the actual decision to close, and there was no accountability from downtown. Discussions included a select few and were held in secret. The people were informed of the final decision in a letter from the archbishop, read at Sunday Mass; the pastors had been told only days before. The "parent" decided, and then told the "children" what would be done.

At first a reactive pattern set in. There were protests, the usual wailing and gnashing of teeth; certainly the chancery office expected that. But as time goes by, there is less and less said. Most people will begin to worship in another parish, many will adjust, a few may decide to leave the church. But the chronic problem of which the closings are a symptom — the nonaccountability of the chancery office, the refusal to share decision making with the people, and the refusal of the people to take control of their own finances — will probably not be pursued to effect any kind of lasting change. And so the pattern will repeat itself.

Abstinence for us demands that we cease to take part in that all-too-familiar dance. First, detachment allows us to step back into our own space (not alone but with our support group and our God). And then we must make the choice not to react in any way — not by worrying, not by turning things over and over in our minds, not by pleasing and easing, not by confronting and protesting.

What do we do instead? We substitute action for reaction. But a caution is in order here. The first things that come to mind when we think "take action," will probably be reactions in disguise. If some action occurred to you because of what just happened, it is probably a reaction. Independent action must be generated by a mind clean of all obsessive/addictive thought of the problem and of our "problem people." Detach, let go, and then get on with what you need to do to be yourself, to be Christian community. What is the next step on your journey to recovery, to wholeness, to personal responsibility, to true Christian living? Take it.

Recovery from codependence means recognizing our limitations and our sick tendencies to exceed those limitations. We have no power to force another person to change, much less a whole institution, but we do have the power to change ourselves. And that alone will create powerful repercussions in all the systems of which we are a part.

Warning: The Victim Mentality Is Self-destructive

In a series of tapes entitled *Recovery* (Minneapolis: The Gentle Press, 1989), Patrick Carnes makes the point that the victim mentality is a primary obstacle to recovery. If we remain focused on the past, the way our family was or is, the way the church was or is, we are saying that we are really helpless. "Of course I do what I do: what choice do I have, coming from or working in this system?" And as long as we maintain that belief, we stand in our own way and effectively prevent any recovery.

Recovering alcoholics have a term, "stinkin' thinkin'," which means wallowing in the mire of negative thoughts, blame, and self-pity. It is regarded as a danger sign, a precursor of a "slip" back into the addiction. The behavior is not limited to alcoholics: we all do this one way or another, with whatever our weakness is. If the boss "chewed us out" and we spent the afternoon nursing our wounds, we might talk ourselves into stopping at the mall on the way home and buying something we don't need or yelling at our spouse or children when we arrive. We might eat or drink more than we should that night, or just sit and do nothing.

If the church power structure does not want to use our talents, we decide to "show them," and not use those talents at all. If the institutional church has hurt us, we get even by dropping out of every kind of faith community. We may even try to disconnect from our own center and from God.

It is a strange, illogical logic that when we feel someone else has hurt us, we proceed to hurt ourselves some more. The longer we feel the victim, the more likely we are to act in hurtful and irresponsible ways. That is addictive thinking. That is codependent thinking. Its purpose is to keep us stuck in the progressive destruction of our addiction.

But we do not have to stay there. We do have a choice. We can either be our own torturers and continue our victimization by reliving it daily, or we can acknowledge that it did occur, grieve the losses we suffered, and move on. We can either remain focused on the past and on someone else and continue to be stuck, or we can focus instead on our own choices and this day that is ours to shape. We can turn our attention to finding something beautiful, something for which we are grateful, something funny or incongruous, and allow those thoughts to heal us.

If we tell ourselves we have few choices because the church administration is stubborn, we allow ourselves only those few choices. And we allow ourselves more self-destructive behavior because, after all, we deserve some "breaks" for having to live with that. Our addiction is in charge and dictating behavior that will ensure it a long reign. When we submit our choices to the narrowness of vision or the bullying tactics of someone else, reacting to what they did ten years ago or this morning, we give ourselves permission to inflict more of the same on ourselves. When we "take a break," and look beyond that, we begin to realize we have options.

The worst part of reactive codependent behavior is that what we choose to do in reaction to a problem is not at all effective in changing or deterring that problem. They are replays of the same actions we have done many times in the past, and they have never been effective. They are almost guaranteed not to be effective in bringing about change. It is precisely for that reason that we codependents feel safe doing them. It is precisely for that reason that no one else ever feels shaken up about them either. The only sure thing about our reactive pattern is this: the longer we do it this way, the longer we do it this way.

The first step out of codependence is abstinence — emotionally detaching from our addiction and refusing to react.

To make any long-term change in our codependent pattern of behavior, we need:

- a new sense of self — empowered, personally responsible

- a new sense of church — freer and more open

- the personal support of others who are trying to live faithfully

- small steps in a positive direction

New Sense of Self: Reclaiming Our Centers

Codependence is cutting out our centers and handing them to someone else: remote control feels normal. As we recover, we will operate by an inner locus of control so that our old codependent behaviors will feel abnormal or sick. The transition is not easy: since we start codependent, we feel we need someone's permission to stop asking permission.

Our own Scriptures provide permission to change and are a ready key to any kind of recovery from institutional codependence. Jesus' message heals: every one of us is beloved of God, cherished by a loving and forgiving Parent. God has gifted each of us with talents and does not intend that we bury those talents and watch those who appear to have more do it all. Every one of us has a unique assortment of abilities and is able to make a unique contribution to God's family and God's world.

It is so hard to believe that we really have contributions to make. It is especially difficult if all we know of ourselves is what we have seen in a broken mirror. We need to find other mirrors — the gospels, other faithful persons with keener vision — that will let us see a truer picture of the treasures that we are.

The way to wholeness and to holiness is becoming the unique self God created us to be. That means looking squarely at all theology that portrays body and spirit as enemies, that says that our thoughts must be sinful because they are human, and recognize that that theology is more gnostic than Christian. Moving toward wholeness means affirming a more ancient biblical sense of body-spirit wholeness. And that cannot be done without reclaiming the centers that we handed to others or to the institutional church.

We need to discover that we do have a right to our own feelings and thoughts and we do have the ability to act. Then we need to define our boundaries, to come to know where our thoughts and feelings place us in relation to significant others around us: love is not the same as becoming some other person.

A word of caution: this chapter is not for the person who would move further into arrogant isolation. It is written for codependents, whose problem is their readiness to hand over every exercise of self-hood in order to maintain a relationship. Codependents need to claim more individuality just to find a healthy balance.

What makes some churches codependent systems is their eleventh commandment against differentiation: thou shalt not think, feel, say, or do anything that was not explicitly directed by thy church. Defining a personal position is very difficult for someone whose lifestyle, job, and personal identity have all been etched in stone.

Defining my position is a quiet, introspective process of getting in touch with my own feelings and giving myself permission to both experience and express them. It means knowing what my opinions are, what my conscience says, and what I need in the way of support. It means looking sceptically at what is expected of me by my denomination and taking personal responsibility for choices about where I am going and why.

As we achieve a clearer sense of self, free of the responsibilities of controlling the uncontrollable, more accepting of who we are as persons, we will gradually replace the first belief, "I am no good," with "I am a worthwhile person deserving of pride." A recovery program, such as the Twelve Steps explained in the next chapter, will enable us to see ourselves apart from our addiction to security or to the power of the institutional church. We will come to find in God and in the community of other recovering people a new basis for self-esteem.

> I imagine the universe as an enormous puzzle. Each of us is a unique and vital piece of that puzzle. No one else has our genes, our life experience; no one is *us*. We are unique! When we are fully ourselves we are that piece.
>
> In an Addictive System, we are trained *not* to be ourselves. We lose touch with ourselves. We reference ourselves externally. We deny who we are. This leaves a hole in the puzzle and a hole in the universe that no one else can fill.
>
> Because we have been living in a system that is an addictive system, we are living in a universe that has many holes. As we begin to claim our lives, our pasts, and our selves, that hole in the universe is filled.
>
> It is in living our own process that we take our place in the universe and the whole system can heal." (Anne Wilson Schaef, *When Society Becomes an Addict*, 150)

New Sense of Healthy Autonomy in Church

Recovery from codependence is growth from a childlike dependence into a healthy adult autonomy. It is taking the responsibility to see that our spiritual needs are met, whether or not we are satisfied with what is being delivered by our denominations. I am not advocating isolationism by any means, but there is an element of self-sufficiency that is an important part of healthy adulthood and that must be there if a community is ever going to achieve healthy *inter*dependence. We need to find that capacity in ourselves, even though we may choose to share the effort with others, even though we may be satisfied with what we are receiving; otherwise we are at risk of giving away our centers — and our values — in order to "guard our supply." The more consciously and actively we pursue these on our own, the better sense of church we will develop, and the more whole and free we will feel.

Young married couples often have emotional fights about holiday traditions because, in their minds, holidays are filed under "the way things are always done." Our concept of church is probably in the same file. It has been there since childhood. It is comfortable. It is also keeping us codependent. Our concept of church has to change if we are ever to reach healthy autonomy. Once we think through the basics of church, the basics of the way of life Jesus shared, we can begin to make thoughtful choices in those directions. (There is more on the process of revisioning in my *Birthing a Living Church*, and I heartily recommend John Meagher's *The Truing of Christianity*.)

Briefly, Jesus did not create a new institution or advocate leaving the established one. He was a good Jew and preached a way of life based on what he identified as the two greatest commandments in all of Jewish law: love God above all and love your neighbor as yourself. His preaching repeated the major points of the Jewish prophets, the heart of the covenant: that fidelity to God (and God is not the same as any institution) and caring for members of the covenant family is more important than power, wealth, or even religious traditions.

Jesus focused on today, in contrast to the future orientation of some members of his tradition. The Jewish community to which Jesus belonged was awaiting a future "day of the Lord." They believed that if they kept the Law and maintained their traditional way of life, the world would eventually convert to their God, would acknowledge that only (their) God is God, and when that happened there would still be a faithful community to show the way. They were maintaining a formalized program of religious practices in anticipation of a future event. (Now, of course, Jewish communities that do keep kosher do so to foster their own awareness of the presence of God in the here and now.)

Jesus was a member of a future-oriented faith community, but he took a different position. He said that the Day of the Lord begins now: treat one another as sisters and brothers, begin to live as daughters and sons of a loving Parent-God, model the peace and harmony that should appear in the "last days," and start now. The Day of the Lord requires that we live peace and justice, right here, right now, not just hope that they will arrive later.

Jesus had little patience for the glory-seeking of his student-disciples, their hopes that he would come to power and that they would enjoy places of distinction. Yet today we take for granted that our churches ought to hold great wealth and property because that "honors Jesus." Which Jesus?

The model of church that many of us grew up with — the religious empire — puts emphasis on property and power, both of which interfere with the call of all Christians, all people of faith, and keep most of us codependent on those who manipulate the property and power. Our goal is small communities of equals that value simple living more than fortunes and kingly robes, that rely on trust in God instead of political clout. We can use as models communities that predate institution and empire, small communities of equals, and make those our primary model of church.

Support

Addiction recovery depends upon meetings, at least one a week, with phone calls and reading in between. Newcomers to Alcoholics Anonymous are instructed to go to ninety meetings in ninety days. Addictive thinking, codependent thinking, is learned in a family, and it is only by immersion in a new family that we can be set free of it. This new family is made up of others who struggle with the same problems and can give honest support from their own similar experiences.

Since the belief that "no one would like me if they knew me as I am" keeps us in a self-destructive frame of mind, the experience of a community of peers who do know us well and still cherish us is an important factor in recovery. The belief that we can never depend on others can be changed by experiences of group members who are there week after week, who help us deal with struggles, grief, or celebration, persons who are willing to be there for us anytime we ask them.

The support groups that we have now are seeds of church. It will take time to know each other well, to remain aware of what is happening in each other's lives, and to share in that deeper dimension of our faith relationship with God. If we are willing to invest that time regularly, weekly or every other week, we can help one another to grow from codependence into joyful awareness of the presence of God and the exercise of responsible discipleship.

Small Steps Instead of the "Quick Fix"

The fourth core belief of the churchaholic is that "organized religion — its rites, its approval, or my connection with it — is my most important need" (see chapter 1). Like young birds in a nest, we open our beaks wide to receive whatever is put in them. But just as it is no one else's responsibility to see that we adults eat a balanced diet or get enough sleep, it is no one else's responsibility to see that we are spiritually fed. It is primarily our own responsibility.

What kinds of activities will fulfill our needs for person-touching-person community, for in-depth spiritual nourishment, for a challenge and an opportunity to do service? And what token forms of those activities have we been accepting instead? We all know what it is to substitute a sugary confection for nutritious food once in a while. And a bit of sugar may be no problem if it is added to a proper diet. But some people ingest it compulsively in place of more important food to create a warm haze and to dull feelings of self-doubt or anxiety. They can become addicted to sugar so that they prefer it to other foods, even though their health may suffer because of it. When we ingest religious confection, it may taste good, may make us feel fed, and may create the warm haze we have come to expect, but it provides no more real nutrition than a lollipop.

Many of us have not taken care to meet our real needs, but instead have settled for words, rituals, or pious practices from organized religion that make us feel good for the moment — a religious "fix." Real adult life does not operate that way. Real satisfaction of needs, satisfaction on a deeper level, usually comes about only by involvement of the whole person in appropriate activities over a long period. If we are to function as Christian adults, we need to give up the "quick fix" and look to long-term endeavors.

One does not simply stop being codependent by an act of the will — it is an addiction — but by slowly, steadily working the program. Taking responsibility for our own spiritual needs will end the addictive belief that the institutional church is our most important need. Taking small steps regularly, every week, in the direction of simple community, spiritual nourishment, and service is much more peace-filled and nourishing, for ourselves and others, than the obsessions and compulsions of church codependence. Once we come to see church that way, we will learn that we are able to survive and live satisfying, well-integrated lives without the "drug of choice."

Recovery begins when it finally dawns on us that our prison is of our own making. After years of believing that we were locked in a dark cell to which someone else had the only key, we stumble upon the secret: the key is on the inside of the door! All we have to do — all we ever had to do — is open the door and walk outside.

As soon as we take that step, we discover that the world outside is not the hell of greater darkness and death that we had feared. When we step into the light, we see for the first time that God is present "whenever two or three gather together." We see that we are connected to many others, though their religious traditions may be very different from our own. We tap into a "new" source of energy, as we sense the creative power of God at work in each of us and in every form of God-centered community. Recovery happens as we discover that we are already free to be the church we are called to be.

13

Church in a Circle:
Insights from the Twelve Steps

The Twelve Steps were composed by two alcoholics and the grace of God. Bill W. and Dr. Bob realized that the only way either would recover was through helping each other. Their program offered the first real possibility of recovery to alcoholics and is still the single greatest tool we possess for use in addictions recovery. The program is simple and comprehensive. It challenges both one's thinking and one's behavior. It removes the burdens of assumed responsibilities, while calling for more fidelity to the responsibilities that are truly one's own. It removes anesthetizing agents and provides in their place a whole new set of coping skills.

The Twelve Steps have become a way of life for recovering alcoholics, narcotics addicts, overeaters, gamblers, sex addicts, and others; for spouses of alcoholics, drug addicts, sex addicts, and others; for co-dependents, adult children of alcoholics, victims of incest; and the list is still growing. (If you are interested in finding a group near you, call a counselor, or call Alcoholics Anonymous, which is listed in the phone book. It may take a few phone calls to find what you want, but the results are worth the effort.)

The steps do not work in isolation: one cannot do them alone and expect the same results. "Working the program" consists of weekly attendance at meetings, phone contact between meetings, and daily meditation. One is never "recovered" from an addiction, but all refer to themselves as "recovering," acknowledging that the inclination will always be there and that recovery is the work of a lifetime.

There are two reasons for church codependents to study the Twelve Step programs. The first and most obvious is that we are caught in the throes of our own addictive relationship with church and can learn from others who have lived with addiction, who have themselves come close to giving up hope, but who have learned to live sanely and serenely in spite of the turmoil that surrounds them.

The second reason may come as a surprise. Those who have attended Twelve Step meetings for a time sometimes find it difficult to continue attending their Sunday church services, because they have found in the program an experience of warm welcome, caring support, and true spirituality that they have never been able to find in their churches.

Some find it difficult to go back to church because they have come to expect straightforward honesty, open communication about real issues, intimacy among members, and mutual support. Some will say, "The churches talk about it, but it really happens here." At Sunday church services, they feel required to keep up a façade of superficial pleasantry, to talk about God without talking about life, and to remain isolated in their own private desperation.

Ernie Hall, speaking at a Ministry Center gathering a couple of years ago, challenged us that our churches ought to be more like AA: rent a hall, have our meetings, live the principles (or as AA members put it, "work the program"). If these quiet little groups can offer hope for recovery from addictions, can work miracles with no titles, no status, no property, and no permanent leaders, and can be more church than church, they offer much that we can learn.

There are two kinds of quests that bring people to Twelve Step work. The first is the search for deliverance from addiction to some substance, like drugs or food, or to some activity, like gambling or sex. These individuals come to a program looking for help to throw off whatever is destroying them and their families. The second is a search for something that will help reach some other person, to fix him or her, to make him or her get well. This is a well-intended but codependent approach to the problem. As church codependents, we are more likely to fit into this second group, and so I will be looking at the Twelve Step program with that in mind. We need to work on shifting the focus from the other to ourselves. While changing ourselves may transform the larger church, that is always beyond our control and depends on other people's choices, not our own.

Twelve Step programs teach the spouses of addicts and other codependents to live sanely in an insane situation, to find serenity whether the addict continues acting out or not. This is accomplished by learning a new way of thinking (recognizing dysfunction, detachment, abstinence from obsessive thinking), a new way of acting, new ways to find support, all described in the last chapter. This "conversion" comes about by living the Twelve Steps.

No Permanent Leaders

Church in the Twelve Step model would be church in a circle: all those in attendance seated as equals in an arrangement that reflects equality, around a circle. The gatherings are for the mutual support of peers, not the instruction of subordinates by an expert. There are no experts in a meeting. There may be persons there who are professionals in medical research or in addictions counselling, who see clients for a fee at other times, but at a meeting that is kept anonymous. Those sitting in that circle have no titles, no special status in the group, only the common denominator of powerlessness in the face of their own addiction and the need to continue to work on their own recovery.

Responsibilities are shared and rotated. Everyone helps to set up and put away chairs and the coffee pot. One person may open the meetings for a month or two, and then pass that responsibility on to someone else. Members take turns sharing their experiences.

Everyone at the meeting both gives and receives. Since each one is working on recovery, no matter how long they have been in the program, there is always something to learn and to share. No matter what the cultural or educational differences, the insights shared can be profound, the growth achieved miraculous. Working with those new to the program reminds "old members" of their own past struggles and enables them to see how far they have come. It also reminds them that they will always be only one drink or codependent "slip" away from misery.

Anonymity

Anonymity is a cornerstone of the program. It is essential to provide a safe place for members to speak, but it is also important in preserving the sense of equality among all present. Only first names are used at meetings, eliminating the power, prestige, or image associated with certain families. There are no names that carry clout, no names that "deserve" special treatment. What brings us together makes us the same: our addiction.

I did an evening presentation in a local parish some ten years ago. The response of those in attendance was positive, but someone came up to me afterward and said that "Mary Smith" did not like something I had said. I did not know who "Mary Smith" was, but the message of the wide eyes, the serious tone, and the emphasis on the name, was that one must not displease Mary Smith. The next day I received a phone call, also informing me that Mary Smith was upset. I asked who Mary Smith was and learned that she and her husband owned the largest store in the area and made the largest contributions to the church.

At Twelve Step meetings, names are not used in a way that can divide or intimidate, but to affirm. At most meetings there is a time for all to introduce themselves and for the group to acknowledge each person by name. Each introduction, "Hi, I'm Tom," is our own statement that here we do not have to maintain an image or have all the answers, we do not have to be responsible for what others say or do, we do not have to answer for the family or the system, but here we can just be ourselves. Hearing the group respond, "Hi, Tom!" reassures us that here, in this place, we are welcomed just as we are, by people who struggle with the same fears and behaviors.

Under the policy of anonymity, we may know less superficial information about the others, but we know more of the real person. There is less "pulling rank" — that is as strictly forbidden in Twelve Step programs as it is in the Gospels — but more true personal presence. We probably will not be totally anonymous in our churches; in neighborhood communities, many will know us. But we can learn to consider ourselves as companions on a journey and can keep our focus on our common need to come together.

No Property

Church communities have sacrificed much to acquire, hold, and maintain property. The continual emphasis on funds is demoralizing; many a church member has been driven away by yet another fund drive. Many professional church workers find it a constant source of frustration that the financial responsibilities of the physical plant consume more of their time and energy than the spiritual growth to which they had hoped to devote their lives. So much of the community's collective energy and resources goes into building and maintaining edifices, while the simple priorities of the gospel get the time and funds that are left.

Twelve Step groups, on the other hand, own no property; they are free from the lure of ownership and power, land and wealth, that has drawn churches away from their original ministries. That freedom keeps the task absolutely clear: we are together to work on recovery.

Each group rents space each week for its meeting, and it is a tradition of the Twelve Step groups that they must pay a modest fee to cover that rent for the sake of their own autonomy, to ensure that they do not become indebted to another interest group, and thereby become the subsidiary or mouthpiece of that group.

To cover the rent and the cost of printed materials, a basket is passed around the circle each meeting, and attendees are invited, not pressured, to contribute one dollar. The primary responsibility of group members is to work the program, to invest themselves in recovery, not to raise money; they are never enjoined to "dig deep into your pockets and give ten dollars" or to sell tickets or play bingo or pledge years of donations for a building. The collection and dispersal of funds remains a small task, clearly secondary to the main work of the group. Again, this maintains the focus and freedom of the group: the primary investment of time and energy is in recovery through spiritual growth and mutual support.

Some will say that proposing that churches let go of ownership is as ludicrous as suggesting that heads of households give no care to providing a living space; it is not. We do not offer a place to sleep: most churches are empty and locked most of the time, so that even those who have no homes are offered no shelter. We need some place to gather as a community, to voice our thanks to God, to share our experiences of God in our lives, and to encourage one another to share our gifts in service. We need just enough space in which to do that, for just as much time as we will use it. A table in a borrowed upper room will do. The aesthetic quality of the space is of much less importance than the gospel-quality of the community that meets there.

It is true that some church communities have managed to own and maintain meeting places without selling their birthright to do so, but in those cases, the communities are small and committed and their priorities are clear. The most important investment of time, energies, and funds goes to the building of community, spirituality, and outreach. Property might be acquired in the service of those goals, but the simplicity of the buildings bespeaks their secondary role. Fundraising does not then become the standard by which one's Christian commitment is measured.

Twelve Step programs remind us it is possible to have real community — support, spiritual nourishment, help for those in need — without real estate. They remind us that we do have other options.

"Church" in the Twelve Step model would no longer refer to the physical structures, buildings with steeples or crosses or stained glass, but, like the name "AA," "church" would denote the weekly gathering of people, wherever that might occur. We are called to build community, not basilicas. We are called to build the reign of God, not our own financial portfolios.

Simple Structure

The center of gravity of the Twelve Step programs is the local meeting. And the meeting is not an end in itself, as it seems to be with many church services, but is a cooperative effort of all present to assist one another in their most important task: working the program toward recovery.

Jesus' message is in complete agreement with the Twelve Step approach — simple priorities, emphasis on working the program, and simple gatherings to support the effort. The gospel is in perfect harmony with the slogans of AA: keep it simple, one day at a time, let go and let God.

In the beginning, there were no popes, no bishops, no clergy. Church was birthed by ordinary people in their homes and in the streets, and everyone was "keeping it simple." Communities met in homes on a weeknight (Sunday was *after* the Sabbath), to visit and share a pot-luck supper, to pray and remember the Lord's daily presence with them, to address the needs of the area and coordinate help. If those are still our priorities, we need just enough structure to accomplish them.

We do not need hierarchy to preserve unity or guard uniformity; it does neither. Many of our programs neither build community, provide authentic spiritual nourishment, nor serve the real needs of real people. They merely keep us busy *at* church, not involved in *being* church.

I described in *Birthing a Living Church* the difference between an exterior structure, an exoskeleton like a shell, and the interior skeleton we humans have. The shell shuts out the world to protect life too fragile to be exposed; many of us have lived in the "wooden womb" of hierarchical structure all our lives. Inner skeletal structure provides strength and support, as well as flexibility, movement, and growth. It is time our small church communities developed their own skeletons so that they did not need to cower in a shell. It is time recovering Christians were birthed and were able to "work their program" all day in all places with a sense of inner strength.

Autonomy is not the same as isolation. There is local networking among the Twelve Step groups, keeping one another aware of the times and places of meetings. Area meetings are announced — attending other meetings is encouraged, not seen as a threat — and sometimes groups cooperate to staff a public information phone line.

Networking is critically important if our churches are to recover. We are coming out of hundreds of years of family dysfunction, refusal to talk about any problems or to any "outsiders." We have been victims of the progressive isolation of dysfunctional family rules: don't talk, don't trust, don't feel. As difficult as it may be, we need to network in councils on every level, one house to several, one tradition to many, local to international, not to coerce or control, but to listen and to share.

We will have to learn not to respond to tension or fear by reaching for a shell, the power or security of institution, but by remembering that God will be with us *at the meeting*, wherever two or three are gathered, to help us live this vision.

Gather from Weakness

Another identifying characteristic of the Twelve Step programs is that the participants come together out of weakness, not out of strength. They know they are not God: they have found the point past which they have no control.

But there is a real freedom in recognizing that limit, a true joy in "letting go and letting God," a natural high in working to accomplish those responsibilities that are truly ours. There is genuine happiness, but the happiness is without any trace of audacity, without the illusion of control that we had before we hit bottom, before we found the program.

The Twelve Steps — A Different Model

The Twelve Steps of Alcoholics Anonymous

1. We admitted that we were powerless over alcohol — that our lives had become unmanageable.

2. Came to believe that a Power greater than ourselves could restore our lives to sanity.

3. Made a decision to turn our will and our lives over to the care of God *as we understood Him.*

4. Made a searching and fearless moral inventory of ourselves.

5. Admitted to God, to ourselves and to another human being the exact nature of our wrongs.

6. Were entirely ready to have God remove all these defects of character.

7. Humbly asked Him to remove our shortcomings.

8. Made a list of all persons we had harmed and became willing to make amends to them all.

9. Made direct amends to such people wherever possible, except when to do so would injure them or others.

10. Continued to take personal inventory and when we were wrong promptly admitted it.

11. Sought through prayer and meditation to improve our conscious contact with God *as we understood Him,* praying only for knowledge of His will for us and the power to carry that out.

12. Having had a spiritual awakening as a result of these steps, we tried to carry this message to others, and to practice these principles in all our affairs.

Alcoholics Anonymous (New York: Alcoholics Anonymous
World Services, 1976), 59.

For our purposes here, as in any program that uses the Twelve Steps, we substitute the word "church" for "alcohol" as our addiction. Bear in mind that one does not do the steps once for all; it is an ongoing process.

Members discuss them weekly, read about them, try to incorporate them into their lives. They work the steps over and over; changing life patterns takes continual effort.

The First Step: Admitting Powerlessness

It would be foolish to write chapters on what has gone wrong with our church families and then to say: "and *this* is the right way to do it; here are all the answers." It was that kind of audacity that got us into trouble in the first place. Quite to the contrary, it is in admitting that we do not know all the answers, but are willing to search together, that we begin to recover.

For most of us, the step before admitting powerlessness was despair: we were trying so hard to rescue or save or fix and found ourselves again and again in the midst of a crisis worse than the last. We tried everything, and then tried it all again, with more energy, more care, more determination, and still, nothing worked! We were obsessed with what we might do next to save the church or save some program or change some policy. We sacrificed our self-esteem, our true ideas, and our personal needs. We rationalized why this person or governing board was not acting responsibly and minimized the damage that was done — "after all, the church is much better than it *was!*" We covered up what would not look good in hopes that something better would come later and make up for it; still, nothing worked! We tolerated lying, and sometimes repeated the lies to others. We tolerated upside-down priorities and blatant injustice in the hope that if we did not say anything negative to the responsible parties, we might be able to "love them into growth" with positive reinforcers; and still, *nothing worked!*

We came to a point where we just threw up our hands in despair and screamed, "God, I give up!" That is the point at which we codependents "hit bottom." That is the moment when we knew in every cell of our bodies that we were truly powerless over the system or particular people or groups within it. And we stopped trying.

Often this is the point at which we came into the program. And for me, the first blessing received in the Twelve Step program was being relieved of the responsibility of trying to fix or control what I could never fix or control — other people and their behavior. I learned that giving up some kinds of efforts is not failure: we do not have the power to change others in the first place.

The movie *War Games* provided me with a good metaphor for Step One. In the film, gifted science students were duped into using their superior intelligence and creativity in a government research project, without being told that the real object of the research was nuclear annihilation. They worked with a computer that had been taught chess and other board games. The computer was programmed to work out potential nuclear strike zones as if nuclear war was just another winnable game. When the students learned the truth about the operation, they turned the tables on their supervisors by introducing the computer to a game that was unwinnable, tic-tac-toe. The computer struggled like a frustrated human — Hollywood is good at anthropomorphism — but finally gave up the effort with this message: "Global thermonuclear war — a very strange game. The only way to win is not to play."

I have thought of that often, not only with regard to the games we play in world politics, but also in the context of the personal games we codependents allow ourselves to be pulled into. We think we can win — this time! We need to learn that once the initiator has put an "X" in the center, any way we play the game we lose. As long as we continue to make our moves — moves that will *surely* save the day — the game will go on as it always has.

Once we admit we are powerless to win and stop playing, our lives can change. We can concentrate instead on other areas where we do have responsibility and can start to get healthy. As we begin to recover, we will model to those around us a healthier way of behaving. Again, this is not to be confused with trying to convince others to change. The focus is on letting go of that drive to influence others and, instead, taking responsibility for our own behavior.

The first step continues with the admission "that our lives had become unmanageable." They may not look unmanageable to others — codependents are great at keeping up appearances — but inside we know they are. Expending tremendous amounts of emotional and physical energy to control what is beyond our power to control, trying to be all things for all people, being hypervigilant to ensure that everyone in the system is doing what they are supposed to be doing or building the perfect case to convince them to change, is more than any prudent human person would undertake. When we continue this ill-advised investment of energy in spite of years of evidence that all such efforts are futile, life does indeed feel out of control and unmanageable.

Some church codependents, like spouses of addicts, are trying to save the institutional church from itself: "We cannot just let it die!" they say. So they clean up after it, make excuses, and hope "they" will wake up and change. We are all enabling. We are getting in the way of others' facing their need to change and denying our own need to change. We are making things worse, and we have to let go.

Codependence has gotten in the way of true faithful living; it has become our clean and quiet way of practicing idolatry and human sacrifice. We waste, bury, throw away so much of our time, energy, and talent, in our adoration of — addiction to — archaic roles, ineffective programs, and those who themselves are addicted to power. Ed Kolacky of Maryknoll, speaking in Baltimore a few years ago, said the waste of talent and energy in our churches is like having all the energy of the Grand Coulee Dam channelled through a single 40-watt bulb. The first step admits that we have wasted our resources on efforts that cannot work, and helps us to free those resources and invest them more wisely.

Pleading and begging for change maintains the very power structure we have been trying to dismantle: we continue to give others our power of choice. Lying and covering up financial and sexual misconduct, particularly the denial of cleric-child sexual abuse and reassignment of those sick clerics to other youth ministries, is a betrayal of our own moral values. We go to any lengths to maintain our own delusion, even knitting new sheep's clothing to cover the wolves. And the lambs they are stalking are our children.

We have lost sight of who we are or which way we are going. We sacrifice honesty for illusion, spirituality for ritual, support for a kind of security that approaches bondage. We trade away intimacy for superficial pleasantry, peace for blind obedience, and responsibility for blissful ignorance. We do what Jesus abhorred, do it in Jesus' name, and proclaim our martyrdom. Life in the church has indeed become unmanageable.

The addicts' delusion is that they are really in control, that they can stop any time, that they act by free choice every time and not by compulsion, that the behavior does not interfere with other areas of life, and that they "can handle it." Not until something breaks through that delusion do substance abusers come to a meeting.

Codependents, on the other hand, often bring the delusion of control with them. Some come because nothing has worked yet to control the addict, but they are hoping the program will tell them the secret that will make that person change. The program does tell them the secret: we are powerless and we have to let go.

Letting go is not selfish, though every codependent part of us will try to say that it is. Calling ourselves selfish just defends the delusion that we have the power to make them change and letting go would deprive them of that assistance. Letting go in an addictive situation is the most genuinely helpful thing we can do for others as well as for ourselves.

Step Two: A Power Greater Than Religion

Step Two says that we "came to believe that a Power greater than our-selves could restore our lives to sanity." What makes religious addiction so difficult to deal with is that God is part of the denial system, the ul-timate guarantor of each one's own religious traditions. Church addicts and codependents do not see any need to change: all compulsive behav-iors that are religious have "God's" stamp of approval on them. Jesus addressed the problem in his time: "You put aside the commandment of God to observe human traditions" (Mark 7:8).

For church codependents, this step might read: we have come to believe that there is a power greater than the institutional church, and that that Power can restore our lives to sanity. Only God is God.

I have found it helpful to distinguish between faith and religion. Faith is the personal relationship we each have with our Creator. That faith relationship should guide and permeate our interactions with other persons and with our earth. Religion, on the other hand, consists of some community with whom we share our values and a set of traditions that assists us in the living of our faith.

If we can come to see that God and the institutional church are not the same and disengage the two from each other, we can start seeing contemporary churches as more or less successful attempts to support their members' faith relationships with God. Some of these attempts began as small prophetic communities, but gradually changed course and went on to become huge, wealthy, politically powerful forces. That does not mean that their earthly reign is God's doing. Some remained small, but have smothered their members. Their tight control is not God's doing either. Most of us have been born into some denomination, but we still have the right and the responsibility to ask if that community actually supports our faith.

Jesus talked about God in simple stories, stories that fit the life experiences of his listeners. In Jesus' teaching there was no heady philosophical debate about the properties or attributes of God.

Those in the program are invited to share their stories of how they have experienced God in their lives and how they are learning to live with a conscious connection with God, but there is no challenging or arguing about how anyone *defines* God.

Step Two does not even use the name "God," but a higher "Power." Some Christians do not like the fact that the Twelve Steps do not specify God or Jesus as the Highest Power. For those who have that reservation, here is something to consider. Many coming into addiction recovery programs grew up in addictive or otherwise dysfunctional homes and are very angry with God. Some children envision God as harsh and as undependable as their parents or as having sanctioned the "disciplinary measures" their parents used. Some have given up on a "God who hurts children" or "allows" them to be hurt. Some addicts and codependents do not believe in God at all, for these and other reasons. Therefore the program is very careful to let all persons acknowledge whatever power they can recognize at the moment as embodying a kindness, healing, and strength greater than theirs, even if that power is the group, so that they can at least let go of having to do everything themselves and can begin the journey of recovery.

Recovery programs can be a first experience of the healing presence of God, however the various members define God. Church, like recovery programs, could be a greater witness to the healing presence of God if we did not make our philosophical differences more important than walking the journey of our own recovery together.

The Third Step: Turn It Over

The third step is one that codependents can have trouble with, because we have not learned the difference between trusting God, or a human friend, and abdicating all power of choice.

I have a mental picture of an old movie in which the chase has ended and the "good guy" has finally cornered the "bad guy." The hero says, "Okay, hand it over," and the crook has to turn over the handgun that was both source and sign of his power. All addiction involves some misunderstanding of the limits of our power. So whether we have been trying to make church members get closer to God by doing everything for them or trying to make church leaders change by petitioning them or trying to make church members docile by withholding information or trying to make God look kindly on us by being unquestioningly obedient to church officials, in the third step we are asked to turn over all illusion of power to God.

This step does not mean that we cease to be responsible persons. It must be understood in the context of the whole program: we admit we cannot force change, we recognize that God is God and we do not have to do it all ourselves, and then, in later steps, we set to work on those things over which we are responsible — our own choices and actions.

Fourth through Twelfth Steps: Reclaiming Our Own Responsibilities

Once we have let go of trying to change others, we can begin to look at those things that truly are our responsibilities. We take a thorough look at our own actions and behavior patterns and identify faults as well as gifts and strengths. We come to see that we are not the worst persons God ever created, needing to be totally dependent on someone else, nor are we saviors who must make others change. These steps remove the fear and compulsion that spur codependence and all other addictive behaviors and allow one to begin a new way of life that is less complicated, less fearful, freer, more honest, more accountable, and much more satisfying.

Step 4. We made a searching and fearless moral inventory. We acknowledge our own part of this dysfunction: in church we are still children who have no other responsibility than to play quietly while "Daddy" or "Mommy" takes care of the larger responsibilities. We have sacrificed our calls as baptized Christians for the illusion of being helpless. We have wasted our talents, ideas, and calls by handing them over to someone else and then trying to convince that person to make good use of them.

We acknowledge how our own dishonesty, even the passive dishonesty of not questioning what is not true, stands in the way of our recovery, and even lessens our conscious connection with God.

Once we have acknowledged where our failings lie, we can begin to take positive steps to be the church we are called to be.

The fourth step is also an opportunity to take a look at those gifts God has given us, gifts that we have overlooked or undervalued because we feel of little importance in church. If we could liberate all those gifts from bondage, we would unleash a tremendous energy for good.

Steps 5, 6, and 7. We admitted to God, to ourselves, and to another human being the exact nature of our wrongs; we were entirely ready to have God remove all these defects of character; and we humbly asked God to remove our shortcomings. This is what confession was originally about — admitting to another community member or members what we have done that has wounded the community or removed us from it. This is our responsibility to ourselves and to one another.

We have been about the business of building an earthly kingdom, actively or passively, in the name of building the kingdom of God. And church families cannot begin to recover until and unless we begin to acknowledge openly the corruption that has gone on in that pursuit. Then we need to ask that those character defects be removed.

Steps 8 and 9. We made a list of all persons we had harmed; and we made amends to those persons except when to do so would cause them more harm. The church has been party to a lot of dishonesty in the past, covering up corruption with the excuse that admitting it would cause "a greater scandal" and unnecessary pain to the faithful. The silence has caused greater harm: it has kept trusting people believing in lies and behaving codependently. These steps should restore mutual accountability in a system that has had little.

In a courageous open letter to the bishops of the United States and Canada, published in the *National Catholic Reporter*, a couple charged that a priest, who was teacher and dormitory monitor to their two sons in a California high school seminary, sexually abused both boys over a long period and used threats to enforce their silence. The priest has been jailed, but there has been no acknowledgment of the offense by local church officials and no offer of assistance of any kind to begin to heal these wounds (Paul and Delia Smith in *NCR*, May 18, 1990). There are many cases like this, where codependent or power-addicted church officials "protect" the church by silence; amends are overdue.

These and other kinds of abuses have not come to light because we who are aware of them say nothing and do nothing. We say we are "helpless." We are not. We owe amends to our community by refusing to hide abuse any longer, by refusing to remain "helpless."

We owe amends to our community and to our world by using those talents we have been hiding, by seizing the opportunities we have to form small communities and to minister to local needs.

We who are church members need to make amends to ourselves for the negative self-image we have accepted. We owe ourselves the nourishment and affirmation we have missed, the joy and shared heartaches of true community, the peace of knowing who we are.

We owe amends to those others whom we have condemned for not following the letter of our man-made religious laws. This is not a surrender to opponents in a war, but a realization that even we are not earning God's affection, and we need not stay "points ahead of the competition."

Step 10. When we were wrong, we promptly admitted it. It is time to promise ourselves that there will be no more cover-ups, by anyone, no more programs for their own sake, no more elevating opinions to the rank of law.

Step 11. We sought to maintain conscious contact with God through daily meditation. We each need to find something that centers our attention on God, to find a quiet place within ourselves, and get in touch with that center each day. This is taking responsibility for our own spirituality, as opposed to expecting someone else to do it for us.

Step 12. We tried to carry this message of spiritual recovery to others. The twelfth step, in the context of the others, is the original inner dynamic of church: church is generated when those who have heard about Jesus' vision of life come together to share stories of their own experiences of living that vision, when those who are aware of their own need for conversion gather with others to "work their program" of ongoing conversion. The original dynamic of church was church in a circle, relying on group support and shared personal experiences at the meetings, as well as daily awareness of God's presence and regular contact among the members.

A life focused on simple community, spirituality, and service is much more peace-filled and nourishing, for ourselves and others, than the obsessions and compulsions of church codependence. Small communities can regenerate what has become old and rigid, blind and hard-of-hearing in institutional religion.

The Twelve Step programs can teach us that community and spirituality do not require a big empire but, on the contrary, require simplicity of life. Only with the power of God can we let go of attempts at control and try to get back to a place of inner quiet where we can hear God and the original call of the gospel to a quiet but radical conversion.

14

Reclaiming Our Centers, Reclaiming Church

I n giving ourselves permission to let go of other persons and events over which we have no control, we begin to recognize the real power we do have:

- power to give and receive true support and nourishment
- power to identify, claim, and use our talents
- power to use our energy for peace and justice
- power to get on with life and to be church

We cannot change just one or two things about the present institutional forms of church with the hope that that will make us all healthy. True recovery will require a rethinking of our entire paradigm of church and of our own roles as responsible agents within it. We must let go of everything in our church experience that allows us to be snug and secure because church is "someone else's job." Those relationships are comforting and predictable — like the ever-faithful warm haze at the bottom of a glass of wine — but they are keeping us stuck in our codependence, stuck in our addiction.

At the same time, wrestling with the big decision — to stay in the institution or leave it — is another diversion that expends energy and keeps us from the work of recovery. It is more important for recovery from codependence that we begin, that we find or create some ongoing church community where we can participate as whole, co-responsible adults — inside, outside, or alongside the institution. As we begin to recover, other answers will become clearer.

Moving the Center of Gravity

We started small, as house communities in which we all knew each other intimately, in which each one's unique talents were appreciated and called upon. Leadership was the work of a team operating within the community of their peers. Church was everyone's job.

We bought the Roman empire at a going-out-of-business sale. We amassed titles, structure, wealth, land, power, and control. We-the-church bought and sold whatever power there was to be had throughout Europe. We damned to hell or executed anyone who disagreed with us. And we claimed that God gave us the empire, that God commissioned church officials to wield the power. We have taken on a hierarchical model, but that was not the legacy of the gospel.

We are stuck, or feel stuck, with this model because of our co-dependence: we believe that we cannot do otherwise because "lay" women and men do not have power in our churches. But when Jesus said to go and spread the message to the ends of the earth, to tell all people about this simple way of seeing and living, he was not talking to a pope and several bishops. He was talking to — commissioning, if you will — working people like ourselves. Church is a work of the common people. It is in our hands.

In a church of adults, all members are responsible for the good of the whole. All are responsible for being church on every level: building community, supporting and caring for the nourishment and growth of others in that community, and extending personal care to the poor and oppressed. All are responsible for every level of decision making, for carrying out their share of the ministries, and for supporting their adult peers in their responsibilities.

Recovery from codependence, developing a healthy, interdependent church community, means moving the center of gravity from a palace in Rome or a mansion in the nearest important city, to the family room of the house down the street. It means believing that wherever two or three are gathered in faith, God is truly there. It means not gathering to complain about what our appointed leaders are or are not doing or how we can change them, but instead gathering to support one another and encourage one another to live the gospel, to take the vision back to our homes and workplaces and out into the streets. It means not waiting for a handful of elite to be church, but letting the energy of the Spirit fill the many so that the incarnation of God's care and presence and ministry is multiplied a hundredfold.

The center of gravity of church can be moved back down to the small core groups, the small communities. Larger bodies — parishes, synods, international affiliations — would then exist as networks of support for the small church communities. Theirs would be a secondary, ancillary role. This is a fundamental shift in the center of church and would necessarily have an impact on every decision that is made on all levels.

Church from the Grassroots

Some want to wait — until the pope says so, until the bishops get together and say so, until at least one bishop takes the initiative and says so. But generating church is a matter of moral imperative: we need to do this so that we can live, so that we can learn to live in peace with each other, with our earth, and with God, and without so much of our energy being depleted by power and codependence.

Would we leave it to our bishops or pope to decide if we should eat — or what or when or under whose supervision? Of course not. Eating is too much at the center of life. Why do we tolerate self-destructive decisions in the matter of church?

If we see the need, the call, to be church as an imperative, then we will take the responsibility that is ours and claim for ourselves what we need for spiritual, emotional, psychological, even mental and physical nourishment: a community of peers under a Higher Power.

The small-community approach to church is qualitatively different from mainline institutional Christianity. It involves the mutual commitment and joint effort of all members to live simply as church, to travel light, focusing on the basics without all the layers of accumulated property and protocol.

In the small-community church, members are covenanted, committed to each other, not just consumers or card-carriers; we are adults sharing the responsibility, not children waiting to be served. There is no priesthood — save the priesthood of Jesus, shared with all believers — and no hierarchy. Instead of one person designated to hold all leadership roles, in any community and for life, all the many necessary gifts are recognized: ability to lead in prayer, to help members be reconciled with each other and with God, to counsel, to preach, to make the business decisions, to visit the sick, to lead song, to bring clothes to the poor, to do story-telling, to communicate the gospel in drama, to preside at Eucharist, to work with the homeless, to prepare food, to care for children. All are commissioned to use their gifts in their respective communities and the communities network together for support and common projects. Duties are shared; all gifts are welcomed and seen as contributing to the good of the whole. We do not sit passively while one person or a team "performs." Clearly, this requires a greater commitment on the part of each member; just as surely, there is greater growth.

We often gather in the context of a meal, but the most nourishing food is the sharing of our lives, the leaven of the gospel as it has been kneaded into a dough of many grains and brought fresh from the oven. We become, with Jesus, bread that is broken and shared around; by the time we break bread at our gathering, we have already been in communion and have really experienced what it is all about. The simplicity and closeness offer a very attractive alternative to those dissatisfied with present arrangements.

We Are Not Alone

We do not need a unanimous vote of our denomination to begin meeting as co-responsible churches. Christianity was originally a lay-based movement, a movement of small communities within Judaism that had a particular focus; they were born out of their parent "church." For years there has been a movement toward small communities within the large denominations of Christianity and Judaism. Some are already living a simpler model of church and have been for years. Edward Schillebeeckx and Johann-Baptist Metz documented the existence of such communities in Europe in 1980. Jose Marins, Leonardo Boff, Guillermo Cook, and others have written on the base community movement in Latin America. Robert and Julia Banks's book *The Church Comes Home* combines their own experiences of the house church movement with reflections on what did and did not work and why. *Birthing a Living Church* cites a number of small, home-based communities around the United States. These books may be helpful tools for those who are interested in starting their own house church. (More information is available in the Suggested Readings section.)

In March 1990 the Salem Community Church in Massachusetts

hosted the Consultation on Base Communities and House Churches. The Salem Community Church is a house church that has been meeting for fourteen years. Those who participated in the consultation are involved in small church communities on three continents and had come from a wide variety of denominations. The consultation allowed the interchange of ideas and encouragement. It established a network that reminds us that, in following the Spirit to new life, we are not alone. What I share here comes out of my own experience of the church at the grassroots, as well as the insights shared by kindred spirits in Salem.

Getting Started

To be church without the debilitating effects of codependence, we have to reclaim our power, the power of all believers, and we have to be church on a scale where everyone involved is responsible.

All that is required to experience basic, non-codependent church, is for someone to pose the question and a few others to respond. The cohesiveness and endurance of any group depend primarily on the hunger of those coming together. We have found that the hungrier we are for community in a simpler, more basic form of church — without the old codependent pattern of "selling ourselves" to get it — the more we will invest ourselves, and that investment is the critical ingredient.

Our small community began and grew more like a relationship than a corporation: we did not put our emphasis on planning a structure, but on listening and presence, and allowed the life to unfold and grow. In beginning any small faith community, it is important to put community-building first, getting to know each other and letting our lives intertwine — ahead of ritual, ahead of theology, ahead of all protocol. To give procedures more importance than people is to duplicate the old rules of family dysfunction. That is not to take lightly the faith that binds us, but to see that faith in a different perspective.

When I was younger I saw our approach to God as some ritual action we do and for which we must follow certain established protocols. The right procedures, those in *our* book, would link us to God; the wrong ones, those used by any other team, simply did not "work." Now that approach seems childish. Now I see the presence of God as a personal presence much larger than all of us, an embrace in which we are held, not a substance we can hold in our hands to dissect and study. Awe and wonder are more appropriate companions than are directories of rites and chants. I cannot control God or deliver God to you by currently correct church etiquette; I can only stand with you in God's presence and try to experience and respond to God's presence and to yours. (Dick Westley's *Theology of Presence* is particularly helpful in this area.)

If we are open to this experience of God's presence, we will discover ways to sign our awareness that allow the signing to flow from the experience. If we eat together or break bread together, we will be able to see these actions as the simple and richly poetic human experiences they have always been. We will see the depth and richness that was there even before they were overladen with long and ornate tributes to our team and to the God-in-our-image who is always rooting for our side.

Thanksgiving: A Eucharistic Mindset

We have found it helpful to begin our community time with each person saying what she or he is most thankful for that week. The victim mentality can keep us locked in a cycle of self-destructive behavior, but the converse is also true: discovering reasons for thankfulness adds to our lives a dimension of hope and well-being, an ability to take good care of ourselves and to share with others.

It is part of a long tradition: prayers of thanksgiving are the heart of the Jewish Passover Seder and the weekly Sabbath suppers that were shared by families or havurah, base community, fellowships. That pattern was familiar to many of the early Christians and continued in the suppers that they shared on Sunday nights. "Eucharist" comes from the Greek word for thanksgiving.

We move from giving thanks into an exchange of what is happening in our lives. This is open, honest, and shared in the context of our belief in a loving God who is present to us, often through one another. We give each other the gift of confidentiality, that what we share is not for public knowledge; that is a lesson from Twelve Step groups.

This kind of exchange is much different from the superficial pleasantries one hears at Sunday worship: "My, how the children have grown!" "Isn't the weather mild for this time of year?" or "How have you been?" without time for an answer. Is there any doubt why those who are really hurting often stop coming to church? It is so difficult to tolerate sweet superficiality when one is bleeding inside.

Rob and Julie Banks make the point that church is about the development of a common life: "when people 'outside' look in, they should see the life of the kingdom in advance." In a small community, we are able to share both our struggles and our discoveries of God, both our searching questions and our dawning understandings. The stories we hear from one another become another set of parables about the daily presence of God, parables that will give us courage when we are floundering ourselves.

There is something rich and emotionally nourishing about sharing food with people who care about each other. It is no accident that the last supper was a supper, no accident that Jesus and his student-disciples grew together by sharing many such meals, and that the early communities of Jesus' followers bonded the same way. In our house, sofas are for curling up and reading books; the best conversations have taken place in the kitchen or at the table.

The small church communities, gathering in many places around the world, often share their faith over a meal or some shared food that signs their covenant relationship. Food is sacramental of our union with one another and God. As we eat together, we have "permission" to talk about deeper things, things that really matter.

Keep It Simple

Can a group get too big? The measure is that each member should be able to know, should actually know, each other member personally, the children as well as the adults, and be able to carry on a meaningful conversation with each one about things that are important to that person. A community that has grown beyond that possibility would be well advised to split into two or more smaller groups more conducive to intimacy. The "sibling" groups can then stay in touch through periodic meetings of representatives to share experiences and problems — networking of local house churches is a blessing — and through larger combined celebrations for major feasts.

It is essential that we keep our new gatherings simple, lest we fall into the traps we are seeking to avoid: making the ritual an end in itself, expecting others to act in our stead, assessing the value of persons in terms of their role in ritual, and giving our centers over to an elite few.

The more time we invest in ritual, the less time and inclination we have to take the gospel into the streets, to touch others' lives with the good news and the caring ministry of Christ. We risk having ritual take the place of life instead of expressing it. Most of us are comfortable using hugs and handshakes, birthday and holiday gifts, Thanksgiving dinner, to ritualize our feelings and convictions. But when those signs become ends in themselves, we are left with the empty commercialization of Christmas and compulsive, superstitious religiosity.

When ritual flows from life, it will be simpler than if it itself is the center. Working people cannot spend hours and days getting ready to get together. Some groups' only preparation is thinking of what they are most thankful for that week. A simple meeting is better than none at all.

For relationship to take precedence over structure and ritual-for-its-own-sake, we have to leave room in our gatherings for reciprocity and spontaneity. Our attention should be on being present to one another and to the God who travels with us, not on a complicated format or the words we say. But the important part of our ritual gestures is the personal restatement of our own ongoing commitments.

When ritual expression becomes so far removed from life that we need lengthy explanations to elucidate the meaning, so foreign to our natural way of acting that we need to rely on others to play the roles because we are inadequate, then we lose the experience of signing and sacramentalizing our own commitments. It is like hiring a "professional" to deliver a hug or a ring. We need a more intimate and transparent form of religious action to say, "I am committed to you and will walk with you as we both are finding God in our lives." The answer is simplicity, back to the basics, so that what we say and do clearly originates in each one of us and so that our action truly is a recommitment.

If we try to reproduce the current format of our denominational assembly, it will inevitably require some members to specialize, to become the experts. We will need to decide who will become the only ones who can "validly" do a particular part of the celebration. Once we have assigned certain people to spend all their church-time on some aspect of worship, we will have also duplicated the institutional problem of making those individuals two-dimensional "God-props," actors who perform a role rather than friends who speak and act primarily from the center of themselves. Most importantly, we will have sacrificed our new understanding that this is a gathering of equals in the Lord.

We will have traded our new vision for the conclusion that we do not count, that only a certain few with special roles in this ritual do count. It follows that we receive value only by turning our centers over to those few. We will be back where we started, back in our codependence.

The basic format of thanksgiving, life experiences, and food can be augmented with readings and the breaking of bread. But thanksgiving, the parables of real life, and food are essential; they should not be allowed to be lost in the religious memorabilia we have saved from our denominational worship. Trying to duplicate all of that destroys our focus and is a quick trip to burnout. It is better to keep responsibilities relatively simple and shared by all, in order to ensure continuity, to prevent burnout, and to recognize the talents and personal value of even the shyest members.

Simplicity is essential to keeping our focus, keeping the center in the center, and not duplicating the problems we are trying to avoid. When we meet, we need to keep it simple so that our actions not only represent events long past, but can also express, or sacramentalize, the ongoing life of this community and our awareness of the presence of God along our continuing journey.

Breaking Bread — Can Personal Presence Be Owned?

For some denominations, the reenactment of the Lord's Supper is a significant part of their coming together as church. Among these churches, the Catholics have made an issue of the fact that they alone enjoy Jesus' *real* presence because of the power held exclusively by their ordained clergy. (Catholics who come to a point where they can no longer tolerate their denomination's politics or priorities often renounce church entirely; they have been taught that no other denomination "counts.") For them, there is no church without the breaking of the bread, and no presence of Christ in that sign without the action of clergy appointed by their institution. For anyone raised in that tradition, any experience of church is measured against that clerical norm — until that norm is rethought.

This is one more power issue, part of the web of codependent relationships in which some are defined as having power and some are defined as having none. We who had none gave up our centers to those who had all and passed on a set of family myths and taboos designed to maintain that unhealthy balance. Things were not done this way in the beginning. The power to be church, the power to celebrate Eucharist, belongs to the whole community. It is time to look carefully at these myths and taboos, to separate the sacred from the codependent, and to reclaim our centers.

The early Christians knew that Jesus was truly with them. They were gifted with Jesus' Spirit, walked with him through the day-to-day process of transforming their lives and the world. When they gathered together, they felt that presence all the more: being among believers heightened their consciousness of that companion they all shared.

When they ate a meal together, their awareness was further sharpened by the remembrance of the meals Jesus had eaten with some of them. (It was eating together, not teaching, that finally alerted the disciples at Emmaus that their traveling companion was Jesus.) For all the early Christians, Jesus was already with them; the breaking of the bread helped them be more aware. There was no clergy. All prayed and supped together, and members of the community led the proceedings.

Our Christian gatherings are supposed to be occasions of increased consciousness of Jesus' continual presence and of the presence of our companions who are church to us. Somewhere along the line, Catholics lost the awareness of Jesus' ongoing presence, saw Eucharist as a church ritual completely separated from the rest of life, and lost any awareness of our own ability and responsibility to gather and remember. Some of us came to consider Jesus' presence one of those commodities over which our religious officials had the only franchise, and we handed over our centers in exchange for what "only they could give," like paying the government to watch a sunrise. Prayerful consciousness, deepened by the experience of genuine interpersonal presence among members, and the sharing of a meal that truly bonds are still values, and should still be part of the dynamic of every Christian communion.

Christians who gather in small communities, in homes or in coffee shops, know that Jesus is with them and have found that breaking bread together in that context is more truly an experience of Jesus' presence for them than it ever was in the institutional settings.

Called to Ministry

Handing off responsibility has kept us codependent. Our small community effort to create a mutually responsible and non-codependent church has to be careful to avoid any temptation to reinvent hierarchy.

The consensus is that in this kind of community there can be no single leader, but all are leaders. Gene Marshall of Dallas explained that all members of his community are considered co-pastors; all are either ex-laity or ex-clergy. Those who had been laity can no longer sit back and be served; they are now responsible for nourishing one another, even caring for those they had formerly regarded as official caregivers. Those who had been clergy had to let go of being responsible for everyone and allow others to get close enough to minister to them. Redefinition of roles is a difficult task for both sides in this time of transition, but the alternative is continued codependence.

If all are leaders, all together must make the decisions. It is the wisdom of every small community I know that all decisions are to be made by consensus. That is not the same as majority rule: every member must be satisfied with the decision or at least be willing to trust the intuition of the others and be able to review the decision later. Grudging acceptance of others' choices threatens unity. If power, fear, and codependence no longer hold members together, a serious effort must be made at achieving operative mutuality.

Jesus taught that we do not have to escape from our life and world to find God, but that the world is the locus for religious action, that life is our point of contact with God. One of the best examples of the gospel message and call to ministry is the parable of the Good Samaritan. A man was robbed, beaten, and left for dead. Those who passed by were the religious aristocracy, on their way to a meeting to discuss muggings along the Jerusalem-Jericho road. The Samaritan was an outcast, a heretic, one who was looked down upon and avoided by the good "church-going" people. He came upon this mugging victim, perceived the urgency of the man's needs as if those needs were his own, and stopped right away to do something. To those looking for a model, Jesus gave an unlikely hero — the religious outsider.

Now we Christians have for ages identified all Jews in the story as the "bad guys" and assumed that the Samaritan represents us. So the story does not challenge us. Look again. What if the "bad guys" are all who are smug in their religion or over-busy with in-house concerns? That puts some members of every religion or of no religion in the roles of the two who passed by. Some members of every religion or of no religion fit the role of the Samaritan. Now the parable challenges every one of us to notice the needs of others, to take some action to help.

The new paradigm of church allows us to shift our focus from "serving the church" to "becoming the church that serves." Church ought not be walled off from life, but allow for a constant flow of energies back and forth between church and social, business, and civic sectors. Once we have come to understand that the gospel is *our* commission, it follows that we are called to use our gifts in service beyond the small community that nourishes us.

That having been said, a house church or coffee shop fellowship will probably not have the resources to launch its own campaign to meet the needs of the local poor. But existing social services welcome volunteers, and house church members will find there opportunities to use their gifts in service as well as to meet and cooperate with members of other small communities.

As we recover from codependence, we will be transforming the meaning of church. We will experience, and others will see, communities in which service, spirituality, and support are more important than politics and power.

Tearing Down the Temples?

Some will see this book as an attempt to tear down the temples that keep our society sane, so I want to address that concern. In an addictive family system, the codependent spouse can spend years trying to change the addict or trying to compensate for crazy behavior. But during those years of well-intentioned perseverance, the codependent spouse is modeling that it is virtuous to give up one's center, to tolerate abuse. The children are being emotionally wounded all the while. They are learning to give their centers away to a substance, a process, or a sick partner, and they are developing destructive patterns that they will then reproduce with their own spouses and children. In the end, many are "lost," one way or another, in spite of the years of hanging on and trying to make things change.

There is a price to pay for exposing our children to years of church codependence and power addiction, for trying to tell them this is virtue and God's will and the way God decided we should be church. They will either see through it and abandon it all as old folks' nonsense, or they will buy into it and give their centers away — and church will continue to reinforce the messages of an addictive society. My fear is that if we do not get back to the basic message and form simpler, healthier communities, if we do not create a healthy alternative, the temples will be cold and empty anyway, and there will be little to be found in the way of true Christian support.

Can we codependents continue to relate to dysfunctional systems without jeopardizing recovery? It is difficult. Can we continue to participate in an institutional church without reverting to codependence? Perhaps we can, as long as that system is not our center of gravity. Perhaps we can, as long as we consciously operate from a different model of church — circular, mutual, interdependent — and as long as we reinforce that different model regularly with experiences of a small, healthy church community, as long as we think, feel, and act from our own centers. Can we continue to function within the system, taking our places as persons-without-centers, without believing that that role defines us, without waiting for permission to change? Each must answer that question alone, with fearless honesty, and that is very difficult to do.

Shame and fear of abandonment keep us in a codependent relationship to church: we depend on church for eternal survival as surely as a child depends on parents for daily survival. Some denominations put shame and fear of abandonment front and center; others leave it over to the side, but it is still the only alternative to institutional conformity. We cannot do anything that would risk a breach in that relationship. So we cut out our centers — our ability to question, to give any legitimacy to our feelings, or to take decisive action — and give them to the church.

In closed and rigid churches, just as in closed and rigid families, no one is allowed to ask questions or talk about problems; those who do are labeled "disloyal" or are silenced. Certain individuals are addicted to power, while others will overlook anything to maintain their passive security. Some cling tenaciously to the old traditions even when those practices violate present values. Some groups are preoccupied with sexual matters to the point of addictive obsession. Some pay more attention to externals, to the white-gloves-on-Sunday appearance, than to the sometimes messy challenges we meet on the Jerusalem-Jericho road. Underneath it all, there is a tendency to cling to church out of shame for our sinfulness and fear of being abandoned by God, to cling to something static because it is secure. These characteristics make many of our churches dysfunctional systems, systems that foster both codependence and addictions, systems that may even need addicted and codependent members to maintain "normal" functioning.

What is the answer? Petition the institution? Save the church? Make the leaders change? The insight from addictions therapy is that those approaches will never work.

We are not responsible for other persons' actions; we do more harm to those persons and to the whole family system by assuming that responsibility. Change cannot happen until we let go.

While we cannot change another person or system, we are responsible for our own actions. The system could not function as it does if we did not tolerate and enable it. We have enjoyed the advantages of our "powerlessness": we treat baptism as a ticket to steerage, not a turn at the watch. We take no risks. We cannot be blamed if things go badly. We never have to use our own gifts and initiative to confront the horrors of physical and spiritual hunger, the threat of nuclear suicide. It is we who must change. Whether we are disturbed at the behavior of our parent churches or disheartened because of our own, the only effective step we can take is to begin today, ourselves, to be the church that we are called to be.

Suggested Readings

Banks, Robert, and Julia Banks. *The Church Comes Home*. Claremont, Calif.: Albatross Books, 1986.

Black, Claudia. *It Will Never Happen to Me*. New York: Ballantine Books, 1981.

Boff, Leonardo. *Ecclesiogenesis: The Base Communities Reinvent the Church*. Maryknoll, N.Y.: Orbis Books, 1986.

Bradshaw, John. *Bradshaw on the Family*. Deerfield Beach, Fla.: Health Communications, 1988.

———. *Healing the Shame that Binds You*. Deerfield Beach, Fla.: Health Communications, 1988.

Carnes, Patrick. *Out of the Shadows: Understanding Sexual Addiction*. Minneapolis: CompCare Publications, 1983.

———. *Contrary to Love*. Minneapolis: CompCare Publications, 1989.

Cermak, Timmen L. *Diagnosing and Treating Co-dependence*. Minneapolis: Johnson Institute, 1986.

Co-Dependency. Deerfield Beach, Fla.: Health Communications, 1988.

Cook, Guillermo. *The Expectation of the Poor: Latin American Base Ecclesial Communities in Protestant Perspective*. Maryknoll, N.Y.: Orbis Books, 1985.

Earle, Ralph, and Gregory Crowe. *Lonely All the Time: Recognizing, Understanding, and Overcoming Sex Addiction*. New York: Philip Lief Group, 1989.

Friedman, Edwin H. *Generation to Generation: Family Process in Church and Synagogue*. New York: Guilford Press, 1985.

Friel, John, and Linda Friel. *Adult Children: The Secrets of Dysfunctional Families*. Deerfield Beach, Fla.: Health Communications, 1988.

Gospels and Acts of the Apostles.

Gramick, Jeannine, ed. *Homosexuality in the Priesthood and the Religious Life*. New York: Crossroad, 1989.

Hoffman, Virginia. *Birthing a Living Church*. New York: Crossroad, 1988.

85469

Marieux, Walter. *The Persecution of the Church in Nazi Germany*. London: Burns and Oates, 1940.

Marins, Jose. *Base Ecclesial Communities: The Church from the Roots*. Quezon City, Philippines: Claretian Publications, 1983.

Meagher, John. *The Truing of Christianity*. New York: Doubleday, 1990.

Miller, Alice. *The Drama of the Gifted Child*. New York: Basic Books, 1981.

———. *For Your Own Good*. New York: Farrar, Straus and Giroux, 1983.

———. *Thou Shalt Not Be Aware*. New York: Farrar, Straus and Giroux, 1984.

Nakken, Craig. *The Addictive Personality: Roots, Rituals, and Recovery*. Center City, Minn.: Hazelden, 1988.

Norwood, Robin. *Women Who Love Too Much*. Los Angeles: J. P. Tarcher, 1986.

Peck, M. Scott. *People of the Lie: The Hope for Healing Human Evil*. New York: Simon and Schuster, 1983.

Schaef, Anne Wilson. *Co-dependency: Misunderstood and Mistreated*. San Francisco: Harper & Row, 1986.

———. *When Society Becomes an Addict*. San Francisco: Harper & Row, 1987.

Schillebeeckx, Edward, and Johann-Baptist Metz. *The Right of a Community to a Priest*. New York: Seabury Press, 1980.

Subby, Robert. *Lost in the Shuffle: The Codependent Reality*. Deerfield Beach, Fla.: Health Communications, 1987.

Wegscheider, Sharon. *Another Chance*. Palo Alto, Calif.: Science and Behavior Books, 1981.

Westley, Dick. *A Theology of Presence*. Mystic, Conn.: Twenty-Third Publications, 1988.

When Christians Meet across North-South Barriers: The Affluent Church Meets Central America. San José, Costa Rica: Centro Evangélico Latinoamericano de Estudios Pastorales (CELEP), 1989.

Wolf, James G. *Gay Priests*. San Francisco: Harper & Row, 1989.